COLLEGE

D1468615

THE
WordPerfect®
BOOK

LEO J. SCANLON

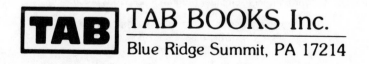

TAB BOOKS Inc.
Blue Ridge Summit, PA 17214

80340

WordPerfect is a trademark of WordPerfect Corporation.
IBM Personal Computer, XT, and AT are trademarks and IBM is a registered trademark of International Business Machines Corporation.
Ashton-Tate and dBASE are registered trademarks of Ashton-Tate.
Lotus and 1-2-3 are registered trademarks of Lotus Development Corporation.
Microsoft and Multiplan are registered trademarks of Microsoft Corporation.
MultiMate Advantage is a trademark and MultiMate is a registered trademark of Multimate International, a subsidiary of Ashton-Tate.
WordStar is a trademark of MicroPro International Corp.

FIRST EDITION
FIRST PRINTING

Copyright © 1986 by Leo J. Scanlon
Printed in the United States of America

Reproduction or publication of the content in any manner, without express permission of the publisher, is prohibited. No liability is assumed with respect to the use of the information herein.

Library of Congress Cataloging in Publication Data

Scanlon, Leo J.
The WordPerfect book.

Includes index.
1. WordPerfect (Computer program)   2. Word processing.
I. Title.
Z52.5.W65S33   1986   652'.5   86-14329
ISBN 0-8306-0857-5
ISBN 0-8306-2757-X (pbk.)

Changes and Updates for Book 2757

We recommend that readers add the following changes and updates so that *The WordPerfect Book* is applicable for Version 4.2, which was released after this book was published.

- Second page of table of contents—Just ahead of the Questions and Answers entry for Chapter 3, insert
  Document Summary 42

- Page 7—On the second line of item 6, put a space between the hyphen and the left parenthesis.

- Page 9—On the third line under Creating a Hard Disk Startup File, put a space between **cd** and **\ wp.**

- Page 9—Replace the three steps at midpage with
1. Type **cd ** and press Enter to put the computer in the root directory (in case it isn't there already).
2. Type **copy con: wp.bat** and Enter.
3. Type **cd \ wp** and Enter.
4. Type **wp %1** and press the F6 function key, then Enter.

- Page 9—The sentence in parentheses under DISK DRIVE NAMES should begin "On an IBM PC AT, the drives are stacked vertically; here, the . . ."

- Page 12—Replace first bullet item with
  - Pressing – (minus) or + moves the cursor to the top or bottom of the screen.

- Page 16—Replace the last sentence of the first paragraph under PRINTING THE LETTER with
  This makes WordPerfect replace the status line with a list of six options: Full Text (1), Page (2), Options (3), Printer Control (4), Type-thru (5), and Preview (6).

- Page 18—Replace the last sentence of the WORKING ON PARAGRAPHS paragraph with
  WordPerfect also has a command that lets you delete a paragraph.

- Page 19—Replace the paragraph at the top and the sentence that follows it with

To delete a paragraph, put the cursor anywhere in it, then press Ctrl and F4 to give a *Move* command. When the Move menu appears, type 2 to select *Paragraph.* (WordPerfect highlights the entire paragraph.) When this menu appears:

1 Cut; 2 Copy; 3 Delete: 0

type 3 for *Delete.* The paragraph disappears and WordPerfect closes the gap.

- Page 20—Replace the first two paragraphs under DELETING SENTENCES AND CLAUSES with these three paragraphs:

Deleting a sentence is just as easy as deleting a paragraph. Simply put the cursor anywhere in it and press Ctrl-F4 for *Move.* When the Move menu appears, type 1 for *Sentence,* then 3 for *Delete.*

Deleting a portion of a sentence is easy to do using Block mode. In the *Deleting a Group of Words* section, you deleted the clause "Believe it or not," by entering Block mode and then selecting the words one at a time by pressing Ctrl and right-arrow repeatedly. There is another, quicker way to select consecutive words for deletion: simply type the character (punctuation mark, letter, or symbol) to which the highlighting should extend.

For example, to delete "Believe it or not," put the cursor on the "B" and enter Block mode (with Alt and F4), then type a comma and press the space bar. By doing that, you would select the entire clause with two keys (comma and space bar) instead of four.

- Page 21—Item 3 under DELETING CONSECUTIVE UNITS should read
  3. To select the rest of the paragraph, press Enter.

- Page 25—Change the second line of the menu to
6 Look; 7 Change Directory; 8 Copy; 9 Word Search; 0 Exit: 6

- Page 26—Replace the text for STARTING WORDPERFECT AFTER A POWER FAILURE with this paragraph:

If you are using WordPerfect and absent-mindedly switch the computer off before doing an Exit operation, or the power goes off during an electrical storm, or someone accidentally dislodges the power cord, WordPerfect will not immediately work when you try to restart it. Instead, WordPerfect displays its copyright screen and asks *Are other copies of WordPerfect currently running? (Y/N).* When this happens, type n for no. WordPerfect then displays its normal starting screen.

- Page 27—Add this sentence to the end of the first paragraph:
To return to editing, type 0 to select Exit.

- Page 29—Just after the Alt-F4 entry in Table 2-1, insert
Ctrl-F4   Move (to delete a sentence, paragraph, or page)

- Page 29—Change the second line of regular text at the bottom to
to the top or bottom of the screen, pressing Home twice and then left-

- Page 29—The line above item 3 should end with "at the bottom of the screen."

- Page 30—Insert this new item 7 and renumber the rest of the list:
7. To delete a sentence, paragraph, or page, put the cursor anywhere in it and press Ctrl and F4 for *Move*. When the Move menu appears, type **1** (Sentence), **2** (Paragraph), or **3** (Page). When WordPerfect highlights the unit, type **3** for Delete.

- Page 32—Replace the menu with
1 2 Tabs; 3 Margins; 4 Spacing; 5 Hyphenation;
6 Align Char: 0

- Page 32—Replace the first complete sentence below the menu with
WordPerfect displays a line of dots, with an *L* at each column position that has a tab.

- Page 34—In Fig. 3-2, add the entry

B - Line Numbering   Off

two lines below the "A" entry.

- Page 34—On the last line, change "shows a dashed page-break line on the screen" to "puts a line of double dashes across the screen".

- Page 41—On the second line of the second paragraph, change "with a [symbol" to "with a { symbol" (i.e., replace the left bracket with a left brace).

- Page 41—On the fourth line of the third paragraph, replace [^] with the word "underscore".

- Page 42—Replace the bullets with the numbers 0 through 8, respectively.

- Page 42—Insert the following new section just ahead of QUESTIONS AND ANSWERS:

DOCUMENT SUMMARY

    WordPerfect lets you put a convenient log form, called a *document summary*, anywhere within your document. The document summary shows the document's name and the date when it was created. It also provides space for you to enter the names of the author and typist, and comments about the document (perhaps why you wrote it or references to other letters to this person.)

To create a document summary, press Ctrl and F5 to give WordPerfect a *Text In/Out* command. When the Document Conversion, Summary and Comments menu appears, type **a** to select *Create/Edit Summary*. When the Document Summary form appears, enter the author's name, the typist's name, and your comments. (To leave a name field blank, simply press Enter to reach the next field.) When you finish, press F7 to return to your document.

Once you have created a document summary, you can obtain it from anywhere in your document by using the procedure I just gave. Although the document summary is part of the document, WordPerfect does not print it.

- Page 43—Insert this item in HINTS AND WARNINGS, and renumber the last two items:

  2. When you enter the tabs form, WordPerfect puts the cursor wherever it was when you gave the Line Format command. To clear all of the tabs, you may have to press Home twice, then left-arrow (to reach the start of the line), before pressing Ctrl-End.

- Page 45—Indent the last line to make it line up with the rest of this list.

- Page 45—Add this new item 13:

13. To create a document summary form or edit an existing one, press Ctrl and F5, then type **a** to select *Create/Edit Summary*.

- Page 46—Add "; it also lists opposites or antonyms." to the end of the next-to-last sentence of the third paragraph.

- Page 49—In the lettered list at the bottom, delete "G. reqeust" and change the lettering on the rest of the entries. However, the last entry (L. after re-lettering) should read "roughcast" instead of "roughest".

- Page 49—In the sentence below the list, replace the bold "h" with a bold "g".

- Page 51—Replace the first sentence under STARTING THE THESAURUS with
WordPerfect's Thesaurus can display synonyms and antonyms for a word on the screen, and replace your word with any in its list. It can also look up synonyms and antonyms for a word that you type.

4

- Page 51—On the next-to-last line, replace *Not a headword* with *Word not found.*

- Page 52—In the second line of the paragraph at the top, replace "adjectives—and puts" with "adjectives—and antonyms, and puts".

- Page 53—Item 8 of Hints and Warnings should begin "With the Thesaurus".

- Page 54—First sentence of #7 should read
WordPerfect's Thesaurus can look up synonyms and antonyms for a word on the screen or one you type, and insert a word from its list in your document.

- Page 54—On the second line of #8, replace *Not a headword* with *Word not found.*

- Page 54—First sentence of #9 should read

If your word is a valid "headword", the Thesaurus lists its synonyms—nouns, verbs, and adjectives—and antonyms, and puts a menu at the bottom of the screen.

- Page 67—In the sentence above the menu, change *Change Options* to *Options*

- Page 68—Replace the last sentence of the first paragraph with
Finally, enter the document name, then the page number(s) you want to print (press Enter to print all pages). For example, to print pages 1 through 3, enter **1-3** or **1,2,3** (with no spaces between them); to print from page 2 to the end, enter **2-**; to print from the beginning to page 6, enter **-6**.

- Page 72—Change menu at the top to
Mark for: 1 ToC; 2 List; 3 Redline; 4 Strikeout;
5 Index; 6 ToA: 0

- Page 76—Begin the second paragraph under MULTICOLUMN MATERIAL with "WordPerfect can handle up to 24 columns".

- Page 77—On the second line, change *Columns On/Off* to *Column On/Off.*

- Page 79—Third sentence in the second Answer should read
Enter the report's name, then enter **20-21** for *Page(s).*

- Page 80—Item 5 should read
5. If you print selected pages of a document using the Print command's *Printer Control* option, you can print to the end by following a page

number with a hyphen. For example, entering **12 –** prints page 12 and every page after it.

- Page 80—In item 6 at the bottom, change "(Change Options)" to "(Options)".

- Page 82—Begin item 21 with "WordPerfect can produce up to 24 columns".

- Page 88—On the first line, change [Tab Set: 25,42] to [Tab Set:L25,L42]. Note that there is no space between the colon and the first "L".

- Page 97—In the first sentence under Closing a Window, ". . . press Shift-F3 to . . ." should be ". . . press Ctrl-F3 to . . ."

- Page 105—Replace the menu at the bottom with
1 Outline; 2 Para #; 3 Redline; 4 Short Form; 5 Index;
6 Other Options: 0

- Page 110—Replace the last two sentences of the first paragraph with To switch numbering styles, give a Mark Text command and type **6** for *Other Options.* When the *Other Mark Text Options* menu appears (see Fig. 7-2), type **1** for Define Paragraph/Outline Numbering.

- Page 110—Replace the first sentence of the second paragraph with When the Paragraph Numbering Definition menu appears, type **1** for Paragraph Numbering, **2** for Outline Numbering, **3** for Legal Numbering, or **4** for Other (to create a style of your own).

- Page 110—On the first line of the third paragraph, change "Paragraph Style" to "Paragraph Numbering". On the first line of the fourth paragraph, change "Legal Style" to "Legal Numbering".
- Page 110—New Fig. 7-2.

Other Mark Text Options

1 - Define Paragraph/Outline Numbering
2 - Define Table of Contents
3 - Define List
4 - Define Table of Authorities
5 - Define Index
6 - Remove all Redline Markings and all Strikeout text from document
7 - Edit Table of Authorities Full Form
8 - Generate Tables and Index

Fig. 7-2. Other Mark Text Options menu.

• Page 111—On the first line of the first complete paragraph, change "the Define option" to "Other Options".

• Page 111—On the next-to-last line of the second paragraph, under Restarting the Numbering, change "Define option" to "Other Options".

• Page 111—Change the menu at the bottom to

Mark for: 1 ToC; 2 List; 3 Redline; 4 Strikeout;
5 Index; 6 ToA: 0

• Page 111—Change step 4 to

4. Type 1 to select ToC (Table of Contents).

• Page 112—Replace the first two sentences of the third-to-last paragraph with

To select the style, begin by pressing Alt-F5 and typing **6** for Other Options. When the Other Mark Text Options menu appears, type **2** for Define Table of Contents.

• Page 113—On the last line of Fig. 7-3, Change "Flush Right Numbers" to "Flush Right Page Numbers".

• Page 113—Replace the first paragraph with

To make WordPerfect generate the table of contents, obtain the Mark Text menu (Alt-F5) and select *Other Options,* then *Generate Tables and Index.* When the screen shows

Existing tables, lists, and indexes will be replaced.
Continue? (Y/N): Y

type **y.** (We'll discuss the *N* option shortly.)

• Page 115—Change the second and third sentences of Defining the Numbering Style to

To select the style, begin by pressing Alt-F5 and typing **6** for Other Options. When the Other Mark Text Options menu appears, type **5** for Define Index, then press Enter.

• Page 115—Generating an Index should begin with

To make WordPerfect generate the index, obtain the Mark Text menu (Alt-F5) and select *Other Options,* then *Generate Tables and Index.* When the screen shows

Existing tables, lists, and index will be replaced.
Continue? (Y/N): Y

• Page 116—Change menu to

Mark for: 1 ToC; 2 List; 3 Redline; 4 Strikeout;
5 Index; 6 ToA: 0

- Page 116—Change the second and third sentences under Defining the Numbering Style to

To select the style, begin by pressing Alt-F5 and typing **6** for Other Options, then **3** for Define List. When *Enter List Number (1-5)* appears, type a number to identify your list.

- Page 117—Generating a list should begin with

To make WordPerfect generate the list, obtain the Mark Text menu (Alt-F5) and select *Other Options,* then *Generate Tables and Index.* When the screen shows

Existing tables, lists, and indexes will be replaced.
Continue? (Y/N): Y

- Page 118—Replace the third paragraph with

Once you have altered a table of contents, index, or list, you must produce an updated version of it. To do this, select *Generate Tables and Index* from the Other Mark Text Options menu. When WordPerfect asks *Existing tables, lists, and indexes will be replaced. Continue?,* type **y,** as usual. This makes WordPerfect delete the old unit and generate a new one.

- Page 119—Replace the menu with

1 Math On; 2 Math Def; 3 Column On/Off; 4 Column Def;
5 Column Display: 0

- Page 120—Replace the menu with

1 Math Off; 2 Calculate; 3 Column On/Off; 4 Column Def;
5 Column Display: 0

- Page 124—Replace the second sentence of item 2 with

To make it restart, use the Other Mark Text Options menu's *Define Paragraph/Outline Numbering* option to select a numbering style (the current style or a different one.)

- Page 126—Replace the second and third sentences of item 6 with

To switch numbering styles, select *Other Options* from the Mark Text Menu, then *Define Paragraph/Outline Numbering.* This is also handy for making WordPerfect restart the numbering from "1".

- Page 126—In item 8, change *Table of Contents* to *ToC.*

- Page 126—Second sentence of item 9 should read

To do this, select *Other Options* from the Mark Text menu, then *Define Table of Contents* from the Other Mark Text Options menu.

- Page 126—Item 10 should read

10. To produce a table of contents, move the cursor to where you want it to appear, then select *Other Options* from the Mark Text menu and *Generate Tables and Index* from the Other Mark Text Options menu.

• Page 126—Second sentence of item 14 should read
To do this, select *Other Options* from the Mark Text menu and *Define Index* from the Other Mark Text Options menu.

• Page 126—Item 15 should read
15. To produce an index, move the cursor to the end of your document, then select *Other Options* from the Mark Text menu and *Generate Tables and Index* from the Other Mark Text Options menu.

• Page 127—Second sentence of item 19 should read
To do this, select *Other Options* from the Mark Text menu, *Define List* from the Other Mark Text Options menu, and enter the list number.

• Page 127—Item 20 should read
20. To produce a list, move the cursor to where you want it to appear, then select *Other Options* from the Mark Text menu and *Generate Tables and Index* from the Other Mark Text Options menu.

• Page 127—Replace item 21 with
21. To update a table of contents, index, or list, repeat the procedures I have just described. When WordPerfect asks *Existing tables, lists, and indexes will be replaced. Continue?*, press Enter or type y.

• Page 130—In the line above the figure, delete the vertical lines around *Sort.*

• Page 149—Replace the Alt-T entries with
Sequence: Shift-F8 1 Home Home Left-arrow Ctrl-End (Define tabs)
Operation: Do a Line Format command to set up new tabs (Shift-F8 1), move to the beginning of the line (Home Home Left-arrow), clear the existing tabs (Ctrl-End), and define new ones.

• Page 157—In the fourth paragraph under *Contents of a Secondary Merge File,* "reserved" (hyphenated in the text) should be "reserve".

• Page 167—Change item 3 in Fig. 11-1 to "Set Screen and Beep Options" and delete item 5.

9

- Page 181—Delete the Escape entry.

- Page 181—The Exit and Save Document entry should read
  Exit and Save Document   F7, Enter, Enter, y, y

- Page 181—Delete the "Extended Tab Set" entry.

- Page 182—Change the Generate entry to
  Generate Tables, Index, and Lists   Alt-F5, 6, 8

- Page 182—Follow the Go (Resume Printing) entry with
  Go To   Ctrl-Home

- Page 182—The two Indent entries should read
  Indent Left   F4
  Indent Left and Right   Shift-F4

- Page 183—Precede the Print entry with
  Preview   Shift-F7, 6

- Page 184—Move the titles Rewrite Screen, Reveal Codes, Right
  Justification, and Rush Print Job up one line, leaving a blank line be-
  tween the Rush Print Job entry and the Save entry.
- Page 184—The Save and Exit entry should read
  Save and Exit   F7, Enter, Enter, y, y

- Page 184—Follow the Tab Set entry with
  Table of Authorities, mark for   Alt-F4, Alt-F5, 6

- Page 184—The Text In/Out entry should read
  Text In/Out   Ctrl-F5, 3 (Retrieve) or 1 (Save)

- Page 194—Insert the entry

  Document summary, 42

22757

10. To produce a table of contents, move the cursor to where you want it to appear, then select *Other Options* from the Mark Text menu and *Generate Tables and Index* from the Other Mark Text Options menu.

- Page 126—Second sentence of item 14 should read

To do this, select *Other Options* from the Mark Text menu and *Define Index* from the Other Mark Text Options menu.

- Page 126—Item 15 should read

15. To produce an index, move the cursor to the end of your document, then select *Other Options* from the Mark Text menu and *Generate Tables and Index* from the Other Mark Text Options menu.

- Page 127—Second sentence of item 19 should read

To do this, select *Other Options* from the Mark Text menu, *Define List* from the Other Mark Text Options menu, and enter the list number.

- Page 127—Item 20 should read

20. To produce a list, move the cursor to where you want it to appear, then select *Other Options* from the Mark Text menu and *Generate Tables and Index* from the Other Mark Text Options menu.

- Page 127—Replace item 21 with

21. To update a table of contents, index, or list, repeat the procedures I have just described. When WordPerfect asks *Existing tables, lists, and indexes will be replaced. Continue?*, press Enter or type y.

- Page 130—In the line above the figure, delete the vertical lines around *Sort.*

- Page 149—Replace the Alt-T entries with

Sequence: Shift-F8 1 Home Home Left-arrow Ctrl-End (Define tabs)

Operation: Do a Line Format command to set up new tabs (Shift-F8 1), move to the beginning of the line (Home Home Left-arrow), clear the existing tabs (Ctrl-End), and define new ones.

- Page 157—In the fourth paragraph under *Contents of a Secondary Merge File,* "reserved" (hyphenated in the text) should be "reserve".

- Page 167—Change item 3 in Fig. 11-1 to "Set Screen and Beep Options" and delete item 5.

- Page 167—In Fig. 11-2:
  1. Please remove all hyphenation.
  2. Delete "E-Tabs," from the Line Format entry.
  3. In the Print Format entry, change "SF Bin" to "SF Bin #".
  4. Change the Mark Text entry to read "Paragraph Number Definition, Table of Authorities Definition".
  5. Add this entry to the end of the list:

Text In/Out   Set Insert Document Summary on Save/Exit

- Page 172—The "Option 1 . . ." line at midpage and the bullet item that follows it should read
  Option 1 lets you convert a WordPerfect document to any of six formats. They are:

- *Revisable - Form - Text* and *Final - Form - Text* are DCA (Document Content Architecture) formats used by large IBM mainframe computers.

- Page 172—In the sentence at the bottom, change "(WordPerfect Secondary Merge)" to "(WordPerfect Secondary Merge to Spreadsheet DIF)".

- Page 172—New Fig. 12-1.

```
1 WordPerfect to another format
2 Revisable-Form-Text (IBM DCA Format) to WordPerfect
3 Navy DIF Standard to WordPerfect
4 WordStar 3.3 to WordPerfect
5 MultiMate 3.22 to WordPerfect
6 Seven-bit transfer format to WordPerfect
7 Mail Merge to WordPerfect Secondary Merge
8 WordPerfect Secondary Merge to Spreadsheet DIF
9 Spreadsheet DIF to WordPerfect Secondary Merge

Enter number of Conversion desired
```

Fig. 12-1. Convert menu

- Page 173—In the third bullet item, delete "(Mail Merge)"; in the fourth, delete "(Spreadsheet DIF)".

- Page 174—In the second complete paragraph, change *Spreadsheet DIF* to *Spreadsheet DIF to WordPerfect Secondary Merge.*

- Page 175—In step 4 at midpage, change *Spreadsheet DIF* to *Spreadsheet DIF to WordPerfect Secondary Merge.*

Contents

6 Revising   83

7 Special Features   104

Introduction

This book is a practical guide to the WordPerfect word processing program. By *practical* I mean that it shows you how to use WordPerfect to perform everyday tasks. It describes WordPerfect from the user's point of view, emphasizing the composition of informal and formal correspondence, reports, form letters, and the revision of text.

The discussion is illustrated with simple yet realistic examples, and each chapter ends with practical hints and warnings and a key point summary. Most chapters also include a series of questions and answers that address common problems.

INTENDED AUDIENCE

This book assumes no prior word processing or computer experience beyond the simple ability to start up your computer. With this in mind, I explain everything in plain English and use technical terms only when absolutely necessary. Furthermore, I move at a relaxed pace and introduce new topics only as they are required to do useful work. I assume that you are primarily concerned with using WordPerfect to simplify your writing tasks, not with learning every possible command or nuance.

WHAT KIND OF COMPUTER SHOULD YOU HAVE?

WordPerfect requires an IBM Personal Computer—regular, extended (XT), or advanced (AT)—with at least 256K memory and either two double-sided floppy disk drives or a floppy disk drive and a hard (fixed) disk. Owners of IBM PC-compatibles and other MS-DOS computers should consult their dealers or Word-Perfect Corporation to determine whether or not WordPerfect will run on their machines.

WHAT THIS BOOK CONTAINS

This book contains 12 chapters. Chapter 1 begins with a general overview of word processing and then describes the features, applications, and requirements of WordPerfect. It also describes how using WordPerfect differs from ordinary typing.

Chapter 2 launches into the actual use of WordPerfect. It describes the methods required for casual jobs such as personal correspondence and household lists. Here you learn how to correct typing errors, divide text into paragraphs, print documents, and save your work on disk.

Chapter 3 discusses the preparation of formal correspondence with stricter and more precise formats. This involves setting margins and tabs, producing proportional spacing, handling multipage letters, numbering pages, underlining, and centering. I also show how to set up tables and how to use abbreviations for material you refer to often.

Chapter 4 describes how to use WordPerfect's built-in Speller to locate and correct spelling errors. It also discusses the use of WordPerfect's Thesaurus to obtain a list of synonyms for a word, and replace the word with a synonym if you choose to do so.

Chapter 5 describes the composition of reports and other longer documents. This involves learning about double-spacing, headers and footers, bold print, subscripts, superscripts, double-underlines, strikeouts, footnotes, and endnotes. I also discuss how to produce backups and how to manage disk space and disk files.

Chapter 6 is concerned with revising text. It explains how to move and copy material and how to use search and replace operations to correct and update documents. I also explain how to work on two documents simultaneously. This involves dividing the screen into *windows*.

Chapter 7 describes some of WordPerfect's special features. It shows how to make WordPerfect number paragraphs automatically and how to make it generate a table of contents, index, or list from words or phrases in a document. I also explain how to perform mathematical operations on rows and columns of numbers and how to draw lines and boxes on the screen. The drawing feature is handy for creating bar charts and forming borders around titles and other text.

Chapter 8 discusses sorting. It explains how to make WordPerfect rearrange lines, paragraphs, or groups of text in increasing or decreasing order, based on criteria you specify.

Chapter 9 describes how to save text and commands you use often in *macros*. Once a macro has been defined, you can make WordPerfect "replay" it at any time.

Chapter 10 shows how to produce form letters. Chapter 11 describes how to tailor WordPerfect to your specific needs.

Chapter 12 discusses how to use WordPerfect with other programs such as spreadsheets (e.g., Lotus'1-2-3) and databases (e.g., Ashton-Tate's dBASE II).

There are two appendixes. Appendix A summarizes WordPerfect's commands. Appendix B summarizes disk operating system (DOS) commands for disk housekeeping.

WHAT YOU WILL LEARN

This book will give you a firm grasp on using WordPerfect to prepare letters, reports, term papers, contracts, legal documents, forms, lists, and memoranda. You will learn how to correct typing errors quickly and easily, set up different page formats, produce special features such as underlining and bold print, generate tables of contents and indexes, and handle tables, equations, quotations, references, and footnotes. In total, this book will teach you how to use WordPerfect to simplify a wide range of everyday writing jobs.

Chapter 1

About Word Processing and WordPerfect

Word processing is the electronic creation of letters, reports, memoranda, articles, books, and other documents without erasures, misspellings, or unsightly corrections. It lets you deal with words as you do in your mind rather than on paper. That is, you can replace them, erase them, insert them, move them, change their appearance, or rearrange them quickly and easily without any fuss or mess. It is as great an advance over even the most elaborate correcting typewriter as that typewriter is over the quill pen.

Thus, even at its simplest level, word processing is a tremendous convenience. You can turn out professional-quality letters, reports, articles, term papers, and manuscripts even if you can't type very well. No more using special correction tape or fluid, cutting and pasting, or trying to insert typing into copies. Instead, you can simply enter your material, make your corrections and changes on a display screen, and print the final copy.

Not only is word processing faster and more convenient than regular typing, but it also gives you much more freedom to change and improve your work. You can correct mistakes easily, even in a nearly final draft that you would never change by hand. You can reorder your ideas, improve your explanations, remove or change repetitive words or phrases, or insert material at the last minute. In short, word processing lets you concentrate on what to say rather than on making it look right. It's even better than having someone type for you, since it's faster, more accurate, and more convenient.

You can do more things with word processing than you could even consider doing manually. For example, you can do the following:

1. Build a library of standard letters, paragraphs, clauses, or other material that you can have ready for immediate use.
2. Insert material from other sources (e.g., contracts, invoices, or financial statements) without retyping.
3. Merge materials to create longer documents.
4. Produce special formats such as underlining, bold print, subscripts, and superscripts.
5. Check an entire document for misspellings, incorrect or obsolete material, repetitions, misuse or overuse of words and phrases, and improper formats. You can also make all the required changes or corrections with simple commands.
6. Automatically add features such as headings, wider or narrower margins, and page numbers.
7. Copy and change documents without destroying the originals or producing work that looks sloppy or unprofessional.
8. Produce customized or personalized form letters, notices, and memoranda that look like original typing.

All these features can dramatically increase both the quantity and quality of your work. Once you have worked with a word processor for a while, going back to an ordinary typewriter would be comparable to living without your automobile, television set, or refrigerator. Word processing is a tremendous advance in convenience, speed, and ease of use.

"But," you may ask, "isn't it difficult to learn? Don't I have to be a computer expert?" The answer to both questions is no. You can become a competent word processor in a relatively short time. You need not understand computers or computer programming any more than you would to operate an automatic teller machine, an electronic cash register, or a calculator.

One of the nicest features of word processing is that you can learn gradually. You need not master every aspect of it to do useful work. You can start by simply using the word processor as a correcting typewriter. Then, as you gain experience and confidence, you can try its more advanced functions. The more you learn, the more you can do, but each step is worthwhile by itself. This step-by-step approach is the one we have taken in this book.

WHAT IS WORDPERFECT?

WordPerfect is a word processing program designed by WordPerfect Corporation (Orem, Utah) for use on an IBM Personal Computer (PC) or an equivalent.

Major Features of WordPerfect

WordPerfect can perform the following tasks:

- Insert or delete characters, words, lines, sentences, or pages of text. A *charac-*

ter is any letter, number, punctuation mark, or other symbol on the keyboard.

- Replace characters.
- Automatically rearrange text after insertions or deletions to produce lines of the proper length.
- Control the format and appearance of a printed document.
- Justify text to create an even right-hand margin.
- Move blocks of text (anything ranging from a word to many pages) anywhere in a document, or even from one document to another.
- Save documents for later use and read them back when needed.
- Search an entire document for characters, words, or phrases.
- Produce underlining, double-underlining, bold print, subscripts, and super-scripts.
- Allow you to abbreviate lengthy phrases, names, addresses, titles, or even entire paragraphs. WordPerfect will expand the abbreviations at your request.
- Number the pages in a document.
- Number paragraphs in any of three predefined styles—Paragraph (e.g., 1.a.i, 1.a.ii), Outline (e.g., 1.A.1, 1.A.2), or Legal (e.g., 1.1.1, 1.1.2)—or in a style you have created.
- Generate a table of contents based on numbered paragraph titles.
- Keep track of footnotes, so that they always remain on the same page as their references.
- Add rows or columns of numbers in tables.
- Draw lines or boxes within a document. This lets you create bar charts and enclose text within boxes.
- Sort lines or paragraphs in a document in ascending or descending order.
- Check a document for spelling errors, and correct those errors.
- Provide synonyms for a selected word from a built-in Thesaurus, and replace the word with a synonym if you request it.
- Display portions of two documents on the screen simultaneously. You can thus look at old correspondence, financial reports, invoices, or contracts. You can also copy significant sections of them into your current work.
- Produce "personalized" form letters from a mailing list.
- Convert files created by other programs for use in WordPerfect documents, or vice versa.

Typical Applications

WordPerfect has many applications. Typical users include the following:

- Managers, business people, and government or other white-collar workers who want to produce memoranda, reports, notices, price lists, schedules, mailings, and formal correspondence.
- Students who want to write assignments, term papers, theses, and dissertations.
- Researchers who want to prepare proposals, articles, studies, forecasts, talks or presentations, and status reports.

- Writers who want to produce articles, essays, scripts, stories, poems, and books.
- Lawyers, bankers, accountants, and other professionals who want to generate contracts, notices, briefs, wills, transcripts, financial statements, and reports.
- Teachers who want to prepare lectures, class rosters, assignments, notes, and tests.

Of course, you can also use WordPerfect at home for letters, invitations, club or organizational mailings, rosters, and other lists, schedules, bulletins, newsletters, notices, and creative or nonfiction writing.

Equipment Required

To use WordPerfect, you need an IBM Personal Computer (or equivalent) with two double-sided floppy disk drives and at least a 256K memory, and a printer. You may also use a computer that has one floppy disk drive and one hard disk drive, such as an IBM PC XT or AT.

Floppy disk drives play thin, flexible magnetic media called *diskettes* or *disks*. These are readily available in computer stores and most office supply stores. A hard disk is a recording mechanism capable of holding much more information than a floppy disk. Disks serve the same purpose as tapes used to record and play back music, language lessons, or dictation.

THE DIFFERENCES FROM REGULAR TYPING

If you are used to working on a standard typewriter, you may be intimidated by all the oddly marked keys on the computer's keyboard. A brief explanation should help you understand what they do.

There are three groups of keys, as shown in Fig. 1-1. The white keys in the center are like those on a typewriter. On the keyboard for the IBM PC and XT,

Fig. 1-1. The IBM Personal Computer keyboard.

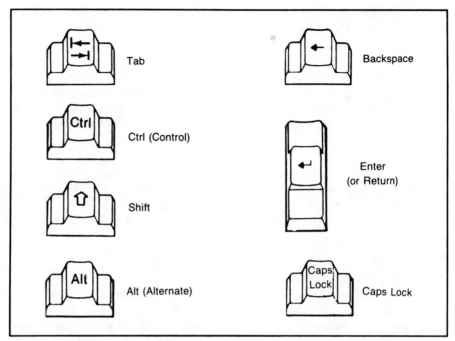

Fig. 1-2. Frequently-used control keys.

however, there is a key marked \ and ¦ between Z and the left-hand Shift key. (Shift is marked with a wide upward-pointing arrow.) If you are a touch typist, be careful to avoid pressing this extra key instead of Shift. On the IBM PC AT keyboard, the \ key is located at the upper right-hand corner of the central key group, so you will not have this problem,.

The white keys also include some extra symbols such as

[ ] { } ` ~ < >

Control Keys

The dark keys on both sides of the central white ones are control keys. They affect other keys or make the computer do something other than just entering a character. Figure 1-2 shows the control keys you will use most often with Word-Perfect.

We have already mentioned the Shift key. The key with the bent left arrow is Enter, the equivalent of Return on a typewriter. On a typewriter, you press Return at the end of each line. When using WordPerfect, you press Enter only at the end of a paragraph or when you want to skip a line. The computer divides normal text into lines automatically. The dark key with both left and right arrows (left of Q) is Tab; it is used to move right, just as on a typewriter.

The key with the left arrow above Enter is the Backspace key. On a typewriter, pressing Backspace moves the carriage or typing element to the left. When using WordPerfect, pressing Backspace not only moves to the preceding character, but deletes it as well.

The Caps Lock key is a handy variation of a shift lock key; it locks in capital letters but *leaves the nonletter keys in lowercase*. Be careful with Caps Lock. Pressing it once locks in capital letters, but pressing it again returns the keyboard to lowercase. The IBM PC AT keyboard has a green indicator that lights when Caps Lock is on, but the PC and XT keyboards do not. Fortunately, WordPerfect provides its own indicator: it shows the abbreviation *POS* at the bottom right-hand corner of the screen.

Of course, you can always press a letter key and see what appears on the screen. One added feature is that when Caps Lock is on, you can press Shift to enter lowercase letters. Nonletter keys always work normally.

Among the other control keys, you will only use Esc (Escape), Ctrl (Control), and Alt (Alternate) with WordPerfect. I describe their functions later.

Numeric Keypad

The keys on the right, shown in Fig. 1-3, are like the keys on a calculator. This set of keys is call a *numeric keypad* because these keys can be used to enter long sequences of numbers, such as item prices, grades, and population figures. The regular number keys in the typewriter section are also available, but they are rather hard to reach.

Note that four of the white keys are marked with arrows. They provide you with a way to move from one place to another on the screen. The Home, End, PgUp (Page Up), and PgDn (Page Down) keys in the keypad, and the + and − keys to the right of it, are also movement keys, but they let you move greater distances than the arrow keys do.

Ins (Insert) and Del (Delete) at the bottom of the keypad are used to replace existing text or remove material from it.

Note that the keys in the numeric keypad have both lowercase and uppercase markings. Pressing the Num Lock key changes these keys from one case to the other. As with Caps Lock, the IBM PC AT has a special green light that indicates which case is active, but the PC and XT keyboards do not. Here again, WordPerfect provides an indicator; it makes *Pos* flash at the bottom right-hand corner of the screen.

Function Keys

The dark keys at the far left are *function keys*, labeled F1 through F10. With WordPerfect, you use these keys to give the computer special commands such as print, indent, or save a document on the disk.

Keyboard Hints

The following hints will help you use the PC keyboard effectively. Be partic-

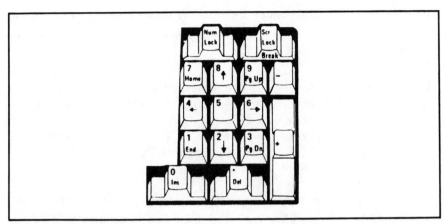

Fig. 1-3. The numeric keypad.

ularly careful if you are an experienced typist; some keys are not where you would expect, and blind reaching will result in a lot of errors. Watch the screen closely until you become accustomed to the keyboard.

1. Note the difference between the space bar on the PC and on a typewriter. Pressing the space bar on the PC actually enters a space; that is, it blanks the current position on the screen. This is different from a typewriter, where the space bar moves the carriage or typing element to the right without affecting the text. The right-arrow key on the PC's numeric keypad is equivalent to the space bar on a typewriter.

2. Always be sure you have Caps Lock and Num Lock off. Fortunately, as we noted, WordPerfect indicates when they are on by showing either a steady *POS* or a flashing *Pos*. If you are getting all capital letters or numbers when you meant to move somewhere on the screen, check the screen and turn the lock off. The usual problem is pressing a lock key by accident, particularly pressing Caps Lock when you meant to press Shift.

3. Be careful when you reach for the Shift keys. Not only is there an extra key between Z and the left-hand Shift, but there are also extra keys at the ends of the space bar (Alt on the left and Caps Lock on the right). Be careful to press Shift, not one of the other nearby keys.

4. Note that Caps Lock is below the right-hand Shift key, not above the left-hand Shift key, as Shift Lock is on most typewriters.

5. Don't reach too far when you intend to press Enter. It's a large key, but there are keys to its right, unlike the situation on most typewriter keyboards.

6. Type symbols carefully. Particularly watch the locations of common ones such as ", -(a lowercase character), and '.

7. Watch what you're doing when you press control keys (Alt, Ctrl, or Shift) and function keys. It's easy to hit the wrong key, and the effects are often very different from what you intended.

The Effects of the Differences Between Word Processing and Typing

Although word processing is similar to typing, there are some differences that affect everyday work:

1. Word processors offer a long list of commands. More capabilities usually mean more commands (as well as more potential errors). Don't try to memorize commands; the common ones will become habits, while you can always look up the less-often used ones in Appendix A of this book, in the WordPerfect manual, or on the keyboard template or Quick Reference card that comes with WordPerfect. WordPerfect will also produce a description of the commands at any time if you press F3, the Help key.

2. What you see on the screen is not necessarily what comes out on the printer. Your printer may not be able to produce subscripts, superscripts, or bold print, even though WordPerfect can show them. It may, on the other hand, have special typefaces and features such as compressed print that you cannot see on the screen. Furthermore, the printer's letters and spacing may look different from the computer's, and your printer may not even be able to produce certain characters. You will become familiar with the differences after a while, but this distinction can create problems.

3. Disks require special treatment. You should save them in their paper jackets when not using them, label them carefully (using only a felt-tip pen), and store them upright in a box or special container. You may turn off the PC with disks in the drives, but *never remove a disk when the computer is using it*. Disks need not be handled like precious jewels, but you should handle them as carefully as your best records or tapes.

HOUSEKEEPING DETAILS

The WordPerfect Installation manual contains a detailed description of how to set up WordPerfect for day-to-day work. For a computer with floppy disk drives, the manual begins by telling you how to prepare, or *format*, six disks to accept data. You can compare formatting a disk with drawing lines on a baseball or football field or marking the origins and axes on a piece of graph paper. That is, formatting prepares the disk for use but does not actually do anything with it.

Once you have formatted the disks, the manual tells you how to use five of them to make working copies of the WordPerfect, Speller, Thesaurus, Printer, and Learning disks. The sixth disk will serve as a data disk; it will be used to store the documents you create with WordPerfect.

For a computer with a hard disk drive, such as an IBM PC XT or PC AT, the Installation manual tells you . . .

1. How to create a special area, or *subdirectory*, on the hard disk to hold Word-Perfect and the documents you create with it. (The Installation manual suggests you name this subdirectory *WP*.)

2. How to copy the contents of the WordPerfect, Speller, and Thesaurus disks, and the wphelp.fil program on the Learning disk, into the WP subdirectory.

Customizing WordPerfect for Your Printer

Any word processing program must allow for the wide variety of printers that are in common use. The Installation manual tells you how to start WordPerfect, and then how to select the program that is appropriate for your printer from those on the Printer disk.

Creating a Hard Disk Startup File

When you turn on a computer that has a hard disk, it always starts in the primary, or *root*, directory. To switch it to the WordPerfect subdirectory, you must first type **cd\wp**. Then, to start WordPerfect, you must type **wp** and press Enter. This requires only a few simple commands, but remembering commands is bothersome. To make your job easier, let's create a short program, or *file* that changes directories and starts WordPerfect when you type **wp** and Enter.

To create the startup file, proceed as follows:

1. Type **copy con: wp.bat** and press Enter.
2. Type **cd\wp** and Enter.
3. Type **wp %1** and press the F6 function key.

DISK DRIVE NAMES

Your computer recognizes its disk drives by specific one-letter names, and you must know these names for some WordPerfect operations. For a PC with two floppy disk drives, the left-hand drive is called A and the right-hand drive is called B. (On an IBM PC AT, the drives are horizontal; here, the top drive is A, while the bottom drive is B.) If your computer has a hard disk, it is called drive C.

Note to Hard Disk Users

From time to time through this book, I direct you to insert a certain disk in drive A or B. If your PC has a hard disk, ignore these instructions. All the programs you need are on the hard disk (drive C), and WordPerfect will automatically store the documents you create on it, too. Therefore, you have to insert a floppy disk into the computer only when you are explicitly copying information to it to create a backup.

Chapter 2

Informal Writing

WordPerfect lets you quickly do informal writing such as notes, personal letters, or shopping lists. In this kind of writing you use the PC much like an ordinary typewriter.

Notes, personal letters, and shopping lists come and go. Most people don't keep copies or use the same thing twice. Other informal documents are worth keeping, such as lists of names and telephone numbers, Christmas card lists, class rosters, or an inventory of your household effects or insured valuables. This chapter shows you how to use WordPerfect for both temporary and permanent documents. Let's start with a letter to a friend.

GETTING STARTED

The procedure for starting WordPerfect depends on what kind of computer you have. If it has only floppy disk drives, put your copy of the WordPerfect disk in drive A, then switch the power on. Otherwise, if your computer has a hard disk, simply switch the power on.

When the computer asks for the date, type it in the form month-day-year, and then press Enter. For example, on May 29, 1986, type **5-29-86**, and then press Enter. When the computer asks for the time, type it in the form hours:minutes and press Enter again. The computer uses the international time standard in which midnight is 0:00 and 11:00 P.M. is 23:00. For example, to set the time to 2:25 P.M., type **14:25** and press Enter.

If your computer has floppy disks, the screen will show A>. Type **b:** and press Enter; then type **a:wp** (**A:Wp** or **a:Wp** will also do, the computer is not particular in this case), and press Enter again. If your computer has a hard disk, type **wp** and press Enter. In either case, entering **wp** makes WordPerfect display its main screen. This is simply a blank screen with

---

Doc 1   Pg 1   Ln 1   *Pos* 10

---

at the bottom.

The large blank area will display the text you enter from the keyboard. In the upper left-hand corner of this area, there appears a blinking underscore. I will refer to this underscore as the *cursor*; it indicates where you are working.

Status Line

The line at the bottom of the screen, called the *status line*, tells you where the cursor is located. It is currently at Page 1, Line 1, Position (column) 10 of Document 1. Of course, these numbers will change as you enter text.

Entering a Letter

It's now time for you to type something. Figure 2-1 shows a sample letter. Don't worry about typing errors; you will soon learn how to correct them. Watch that you don't press Caps Lock accidentally, however; if you do, WordPerfect will capitalize the Position abbreviation (change it from *Pos* to *POS*).

To begin, type the date. The first letter will appear at the cursor's location in the upper left-hand corner of the screen. The cursor moves right automatically as you type. Now press Enter. The computer's Enter key is like the Return key on a typewriter; that is, it moves the typing location indicator (cursor) to the beginning of the next line.

Since the salutation starts two lines down from the date, press Enter again, then type **Dear John:**. Now press Enter twice more to reach the line where the body of the letter begins.

Now type the body, but *don't press Enter at the end of each line*. This is a major advantage of word processing over ordinary typing. WordPerfect keeps track of how long each line is and brings the cursor down to the next line automatically. Press Enter only when you reach the end of a paragraph or want to skip a line.

After you type the close (**All the best,**), press Enter four times to reach the line for your name, then type it, and press Enter once more.

CORRECTING ERRORS

You probably made some mistakes when you typed the letter. Fortunately,

```
May 11, 1986

Dear John:

Believe it or not, I'm writing this letter on my IBM Personal
Computer!  I bought a word processing program called WordPerfect
that lets me use the PC just like a typewriter.  Since this is my
first try at using it, I can't tell you how easy it actually is,
but so far so good.

Pat and I want to invite you, Sandra, and Robby to our new summer
cabin by Bender Lake.  To paraphrase an old joke, when can you
drop in?  Write soon.

All the best,


(Type your name here)
```

Fig. 2-1. A sample letter to a friend.

correcting errors is easy with word processing. After all, the errors are only on the screen, not imprinted on paper.

To correct an error, you must first move the cursor to it. Do this with the arrow keys and the other keys on the numeric keypad. Remember that you can't use the space bar to move over material, since it will actually enter spaces.

Moving the Cursor

As you could probably guess, the arrow keys on the numeric keypad move the cursor in the direction they point—that is, right (6), left (4), up (8), and down (2). The arrow keys only move the cursor a character at a time horizontally or a line at a time vertically. To move greater distances, you can use some other keypad keys, as follows:

- Pressing – (minus) or + moves the cursor to the beginning or end of the text on the screen.
- Pressing Home twice, then the left-arrow key, moves it to the beginning of the current line.
- Pressing End moves it to the end of the current line.

Figure 2-2 shows the arrangement of these cursor-moving keys. Be sure Num Lock is off when you use these keys. If it is on, WordPerfect will make *Pos* flash at the bottom right-hand corner of the screen. In that case, press Num Lock to turn it off.

Not only do the arrow keys have directions marked on them, but they are also placed according to the way they point. That is, the up-arrow key is above the others, the left-arrow key is to the left, and so on. These keys *repeat*—they keep the cursor moving as long as you hold them down.

If you have followed directions so far, the letter is on the screen, and the cursor is on the line below your name. Press the up-arrow key. It will move the cursor up one line each time you press it. Move up a line or two and then keep your finger on the key until the cursor reaches the top (date) line. The cursor will not move higher.

Now press the down-arrow key until the cursor is on the first line of the second paragraph—the line that starts with "Pat and I". (If the cursor moves too far, use the up-arrow key to backtrack.)

Suppose we really meant to type Pam instead of Pat. Let's see how to correct this mistake.

Changing Characters

Changing a character with WordPerfect is like changing one with a correcting typewriter: move the cursor to it, delete it, then type the new character. Therefore, to change Pat to Pam, use the arrow keys to move the cursor to the t in Pat. Now press the Del (Delete) key (below the numeric keypad) and type m. The t has vanished and m is in its place. If you made any other one-character mistakes, correct them now.

It's just as easy to change several characters. Simply move the cursor to where the changes begin, press Del once for each character you want to delete, and then type the new characters. Of course, you can also use Del alone to simply erase extra characters. This includes spaces; remember that a space is a character— it's the "invisible man" of the character world.

Inserting Characters

To insert characters, simply move the cursor just to the right of (that is, just beyond) where you want the insertion, then type the new characters. They will

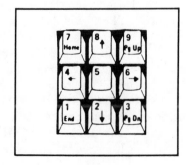

Fig. 2-2. Cursor-moving keys. Courtesy International Business Machines Corp.

be inserted just left of the cursor. If the additional characters make the line too long, WordPerfect automatically moves the excess to the next line and rearranges the paragraph to make every line the proper length.

To see how insertion and deletion work, let's try them on our example letter. Specifically, let's assume that Sandra should be Saundra.

To change Sandra to Saundra, move the cursor to the first line of the second paragraph, then right to the n in Sandra. (Note that we place the cursor just beyond where we want the insertion.) Now press u. The extra letter makes the line too long, so when you move the cursor to any other line, WordPerfect automatically moves the word "summer" to the next line and rearranges the rest of the paragraph as follows:

Pam and I want to invite you, Saundra, and Robby to our new summer cabin by Bender Lake. To paraphrase an old joke, when can you drop in? Write soon.

If you see other words that have too many or too few characters, make the appropriate insertions and deletions in a similar manner.

Deleting to the Left

You can delete a character you just typed by pressing the Backspace key, the dark left-arrow key above Enter. Pressing Backspace deletes the character just to the left of the cursor. Note how this differs from Del, which deletes the character at the cursor position. Del is more natural, but Backspace is handy because the cursor moves when you delete. Suppose, for example, you meant to type r, but when you look at the screen, you see t instead. You can't just press Del, since the cursor has moved to the right, but you *can* press Backspace and then r.

Typeover

To change two or three consecutive characters, you can press the Ins key to put WordPerfect in the *Typeover* mode. In this mode, WordPerfect automatically replaces old characters with ones you type. It also reminds you that Typeover is active by showing *Typeover* at the beginning of the status line. WordPerfect stays in the Typeover mode until you press Ins again.

Typeover is handy for corrections that are about the same length as the originals, but quite different. For example, suppose you type "He can precede" instead of "He may proceed". To correct this error, move the cursor to the "c" in "can", press Ins to put WordPerfect in Typeover mode, type **may proceed**, then press Ins again to put WordPerfect back in the Insert mode. Sometimes this is quicker and more natural than inserting and deleting.

CHANGING WORDS

You can handle words as sequences of characters—that is, insert or delete them a character at a time. WordPerfect, however, simplifies this by providing ways to handle a word, rather than a character, at a time.

Deleting Words

To delete a word, put the cursor just beyond it or on any character in it, then hold Ctrl down and press Backspace. If the deletion makes the line too short, WordPerfect automatically rearranges the rest of the paragraph.

To see how this works, let's delete the word new from the second paragraph of our example letter. To do this, move the cursor to the n, then press Ctrl and Backspace. The entire word disappears. Note also how WordPerfect rearranges the rest of the paragraph. Now it has the following form:

> Pam and I want to invite you, Saundra, and Robby to our summer cabin by Bender Lake. To paraphrase an old joke, when can you drop in? Write soon.

Moving the Cursor a Word at a Time

You can also use the Ctrl key to move the cursor quickly. Pressing Ctrl and left-arrow together moves it one word to the left, while pressing Ctrl and right-arrow together moves it one word to the right. Like the arrow keys, these key combinations repeat; that is, the cursor keeps moving as long as you hold them down.

Deleting a Group of Words

Suppose you want to delete several consecutive words. You could delete them one at a time with Ctrl and Backspace, but there is a way to remove all of them in one operation.

To select a group of consecutive words, press Alt and F4 to put WordPerfect in the *Block* mode, then press Ctrl and right-arrow to move the cursor right (or Ctrl and left-arrow to move it left) once for each word. As the cursor moves, WordPerfect highlights each word it passes. When the highlighting covers all the words you want to delete, press the Del key.

Since deleting a block of words is a drastic act, WordPerfect gives you a chance to change your mind. It displays *Delete Block? (Y/N) N* on the status line. The final *N* here is WordPerfect's guess as to what you want to do; for safety's sake, it assumes you don't want to perform the deletion. To delete the block, press y; to leave it intact and cancel the delete operation, press n or Enter.

To see how this works, let's remove the clause "Believe it or not," from our example letter. To do this, move the cursor to the "B" in "Believe" and then press Alt and F4 to put WordPerfect in the Block mode. The words *Block on* appear, flashing on the status line. Now press Ctrl and right-arrow four times to select "Believe ", "it ", "or ", and "not, ". (Note that WordPerfect thinks the comma is part of the word not.) Since the entire clause is now highlighted, press Del and y to delete it.

As usual, when you move the cursor off that line, WordPerfect rearranges the rest of the paragraph. Its final form is as follows:

I'm writing this letter on my IBM Personal Computer! I bought a word processing program called WordPerfect that lets me use the PC just like a typewriter. Since this is my first try at using it, I can't tell you how easy it actually is, but so far so good.

PRINTING THE LETTER

Now that we are done editing the letter, let's see how it looks in print. To begin, turn your printer on, and if necessary, switch it to the *on-line* or *selected* mode. Now, to choose WordPerfect's Print command, hold Shift down and press the F7 function key. This makes WordPerfect replace the status line with a list of five options: Full Text (1), Page (2), Change Options (3), Printer Control (4), and Type-thru (5).

To print your letter, type 2 to select Page. (Note that since the letter is only one page long, selecting Full Text—i.e., the entire document—for printing would work just as well.) WordPerfect shows * *Please Wait* * at the bottom of the screen, then prints the letter. If you did everything correctly so far, the letter should look like the one shown in Fig. 2-3.

Note that the text is printed in *justified* form (with an even right-hand margin), even though it has a ragged right margin on the screen. WordPerfect always prints text justified unless you tell it otherwise. We describe how to print without justification later in this book.

Print Margins

Besides justifying text, WordPerfect automatically provides one-inch margins at the top and along the left and right sides. If your copy of the letter has a wider or narrower top margin, move the paper downward or upward to compensate. Similarly, if the copy has a left-hand margin that is more or less than one inch, move the printer's paper-feed sprockets to the left or right.

Now that you have a printed copy, you can examine it for mistakes. If you

```
May 11, 1986

Dear John:

I'm writing this letter on my IBM Personal Computer!  I bought a
word processing program called WordPerfect that lets me use the
PC just like a typewriter.  Since this is my first try at using
it, I can't tell you how easy it actually is, but so far so good.

Pam and I want to invite you, Saundra, and Robby to our summer
cabin by Bender Lake.  To paraphrase an old joke, when can you
drop in?  Write soon.

All the best,


(Type your name here)
```

Fig. 2-3. The printed form of sample letter.

see any, correct them and print the letter again. To start a new project, however, you must first clear the screen.

Clearing the Screen

To clear the screen, press F7 to select the Exit command. When the screen shows

Save Document? (Y/N) Y

type n for No. WordPerfect then wants to know whether you're done working with it. It asks

Exit WP? (Y/N) N

Type n or press Enter to stay in WordPerfect. The screen now looks just as it did when we started: blank, with the cursor in the upper left-hand corner.

PREPARING A LIST

Now you can start a new project. This time, let's make a list of names and telephone numbers and save it on disk. Before continuing, insert your data disk in drive B. Now enter the sample telephone list shown in Fig. 2-4.

CHANGING LINES

Although we did not need this ability for our short letter, WordPerfect can also handle lines at one time. The most likely occasion for changing an entire line is when you are editing a list of items, such as a recipe, a telephone list, or a class roster.

To insert a line, put the cursor at the beginning of the line that follows where you want the insertion to appear, then enter the new line and press Enter. The old line moves right as you type, then Enter moves it down, separating it from the new line.

Let's add the local library's telephone number to our example list. Specifically, we want to put *Library 555-2738* between the entries for Lois Lane and Pam Michelle. To add the line, move the cursor to the "M" in "Michelle", enter the new line, then press Enter.

To delete a line, put the cursor at the beginning of it, then press Ctrl and End. The line disappears, but there is a gap where it used to be. (Apparently, WordPerfect assumes that you want to replace the old line with a new one.) To close the gap, press Del.

WORKING ON PARAGRAPHS

WordPerfect identifies paragraphs by *Enters* (the results of pressing the Enter key). Thus you can use Enters to insert a paragraph or divide one into two. WordPerfect also lets you select a paragraph (or a portion of one) for deletion by using the Block mode.

Inserting and Deleting Paragraphs

To insert a paragraph, put the cursor at the end of the line where you want the insertion, and then press Enter. WordPerfect opens a one-line gap into which

```
Brown, Byron 356-7732
Carlson, Joan 753-6844
Edgewood, Peter 847-3896
Grayson, Dr. Leonard 931-5410
Lane, Lois 557-1332
Michelle, Pam 602-5419
Raymond, Morris 705-5537
Tyner, Mavis 965-2694
```

Fig. 2-4. A telephone list.

you can type the new paragraph. (Don't press Enter after this paragraph unless you want to insert another one.)

To delete a paragraph, put the cursor on the first character and then do the following:

1. Press Alt and F4 to put WordPerfect in the Block mode.
2. Press Enter to highlight the rest of the paragraph.
3. Press Del.
4. When WordPerfect asks *Delete Block? (Y/N) N*, type y.

The paragraph disappears and WordPerfect closes the gap.

Dividing Paragraphs

Pressing the Enter key tells WordPerfect to begin a new paragraph. Therefore, to divide a paragraph, simply move the cursor to the character where you want the new paragraph to begin, and then press Enter. WordPerfect moves the rest of the paragraph down one line and rearranges it to form a properly spaced new paragraph.

For example, suppose you have accidentally combined two unrelated topics in a single paragraph. Perhaps you wrote

> Jim and Ellen stopped over for bridge last night. Jim is a mediocre player, but Ellen plays like a professional. Of course, they beat us easily, as usual. Tom had a cold, but he's almost totally recovered now. We expect to send him back to school Tuesday.

To put the two subjects (bridge and Tom's cold) into separate paragraphs, you would move the cursor to the T in Tom and then press Enter. Your text now looks like this:

> Jim and Ellen stopped over for bridge last night. Jim is a mediocre player, but Ellen plays like a professional. Of course, they beat us easily, as usual.
> Tom had a cold, but he's almost totally recovered now. We expect to send him back to school Tuesday.

Press Enter again to insert a blank line between the paragraphs.

Combining Paragraphs

To combine two paragraphs, move the cursor to the space after the final sentence of the first paragraph, press the space bar twice to put two spaces between the sentences, and then press Del. The two paragraphs are now one. All we did was delete the Enters between them.

Moving Between Paragraphs

To move the cursor a paragraph ahead, give WordPerfect a "Go to" command by pressing Ctrl and Home simultaneously. This makes the status line show *Go to*, which means that WordPerfect is asking "Go to what?" Since paragraphs are separated by an Enter, press Enter. WordPerfect puts the cursor just past the next Enter; that is, it puts the cursor at the beginning of the next paragraph.

DELETING SENTENCES AND CLAUSES

In the preceding section, I described the use of the Block mode to select a paragraph for deletion. This involves simply putting WordPerfect into Block mode (by pressing Alt and F4) and then pressing Enter to select the rest of the paragraph. The reason pressing Enter selects the paragraph is that in Block mode, WordPerfect automatically extends the highlighting to the next character you type. This feature allows you to select a sentence (or a portion of one) by typing the last deletion character—a punctuation mark, letter, or symbol.

For example, in the *Deleting a Group of Words* section, you deleted the clause "Believe it or not," by entering Block mode and then selecting the words one at a time by pressing Ctrl and right-arrow repeatedly. It would have been quicker and easier to put the cursor on the B, enter Block mode, type a comma, and press the space bar. By doing that, you would select the entire clause with two keys (comma and space bar) instead of four.

Entering end characters to extend the highlighting is convenient if it doesn't involve too much work to reach them. If, however, there are many such characters between where the cursor is and where you want it to end up, you should probably stick with using the numeric keypad keys to extend the highlighting. For example, selecting the sentence

Dr. George R. Hardy of Adams Ave. Clinic in St. Louis, Mo. charges only $2.50 for a house call.

would require you to press the period key seven times to reach the period at the end. It is faster and easier to move the cursor there directly using the keypad keys (say, down-arrow to select the first line and then End to reach the end of the second line).

DELETING CONSECUTIVE UNITS

You can also use Block mode to select *consecutive* units (words, lines, paragraphs, or sentences) for deletion. To begin, put the cursor on the first character to be deleted, then press Alt and F4 to put WordPerfect in Block mode. After that, select the first unit you want to delete, and then use a similar approach to select the next one, and so on. When all of the units you want to delete are highlighted, press Del to start the deletion operation and, when WordPerfect asks *Delete Block? (Y/N) N*, type **y** to complete it.

Once WordPerfect is in Block mode, you can do any of the following things to select consecutive units:

1. To select the next word, press Ctrl and right-arrow.
2. To select the next line, press down-arrow to reach it, and then press End to extend the highlighting to the end of that line.
3. To select the next paragraph, press Enter.
4. To select the next sentence or clause, type the character at the end of it.

RESTORING DELETED TEXT

So far, we have discussed several ways you can delete text with WordPerfect. Recall that you can delete a character by pressing Del, a word by pressing Ctrl-Backspace, a line by pressing Ctrl-End, and a sentence, clause, or paragraph by selecting it in Block mode and pressing Del. When you delete text using any of these methods, WordPerfect does not immediately discard it, but instead temporarily saves it in the computer's memory. In fact, WordPerfect keeps text from the last *three* deletions in memory!

To recycle deleted text, simply move the cursor to where you want it to appear and press the F1 (Cancel) key. This makes WordPerfect display the text, shaded, at the cursor position and show the following option list at the bottom of the screen:

Undelete 1 Restore; 2 Show Previous Deletion: 0

Now you have three choices: to undelete, or restore, the shaded text, type **1**; to show the text you deleted before this deletion, type **2**; to return to editing (if, say, you pressed F1 by mistake), press Enter.

As an illustration of restoring deleted text, let's suppose you absent-mindedly transposed Raymond Morris' name in the telephone list, entering *Raymond, Morris* instead of *Morris, Raymond*, so you want to switch these words. To do this, move the cursor to the "R" in "Raymond," then press Ctrl and Backspace. "Raymond," disappears. Now move the cursor to the space after *Morris*, and type a comma and a space. The cursor is now where we want *Raymond* to appear, so press F1 and then 1, to retrieve "Raymond," from memory and insert it. (Note that the word is still in memory, so you could use it again later if you wanted to.) Finally, press Backspace twice to delete the extra space and the comma.

SAVING A DOCUMENT ON DISK

To save the telephone list on disk, press the F10 key to give WordPerfect a Save command. Now WordPerfect displays

Document to be Saved:

and waits for you to enter a name for the list. This is necessary because eventually your disk will hold several documents, and you need some way to identify them.

Document Names

Documents (*files*) on disks can have names up to eight characters long, and can be followed by an optional *extension* consisting of a period and up to three more characters. These names should be meaningful, easy to read and type, and easy to tell apart. They may consist of letters, numbers (0-9), or any of the following symbols:

$ & # @ ! % ' – ( ) { } — ` ^

You may use either capital or lowercase letters; WordPerfect treats them as identical. Beware the obvious problems with O (letter) and 0 (zero), and I (letter) and 1 (number). Those who use filenames like IO01I0 will get the fate they deserve.

Since the document here is a telephone list, type **phone.lst** for its filename; then press Enter. When you do this, the red light on drive B comes on and the drive makes a whirring sound. WordPerfect also displays

Saving B:\PHONE.LST

on the status line. When WordPerfect finishes (be patient—this will take a while if the document is long), it waits for you to resume editing.

Canceling a Save Operation

If you accidentally pressed F10 when you meant to press, say, Shift, you can cancel the Save operation by pressing F1 (Cancel). This makes WordPerfect remove the *Document to be Saved:* message and return to editing. F1 is handy for backing out of many operations, including just about any of them that displays a message.

EDITING A DISK DOCUMENT

Once you have documents on the disk, you will probably spend more time working on them than creating new ones. To retrieve a document from disk, press Shift and F10 to give WordPerfect a Retrieve command. When WordPerfect displays

Document to be Retrieved:

enter the file's name and then press Enter.

WordPerfect now reads the document into the computer and displays it on the screen as if you had just entered it.

Removing the Telephone List

To see how this works, let's remove the telephone list from the screen and then retrieve it from disk. To begin, press F7 to do an Exit operation. When Word-Perfect displays

Save Document? (Y/N) Y

type **n** (we just saved the list—no need to save it again). The next prompt,

Exit WP? (Y/N) N

asks whether or not you want to leave WordPerfect. Since we want to retrieve a document, press Enter to accept *N* for No. WordPerfect clears the screen and waits for you to enter another command.

Retrieving the List

To obtain the PHONE.LST document, press Shift and F10 to give Word-Perfect a Retrieve command. When the screen shows *Document to be Retrieved:*, type **phone.lst** and press Enter. WordPerfect now copies the telephone list from the disk into the computer and displays it on the screen (the original is still on the disk). For practice, insert **Evans, Tom 555-1348** and **Storr, Kim 489-7277** at the proper places in the list.

Saving the List

At this point, you will want to save the new list on disk. You could give Word-Perfect a Save command (by pressing F10) and continue editing the list, but instead, let's suppose you want to work on another document on the disk. To do this, you must clear the screen and then retrieve the new document. Proceed as follows:

1. Press F7 to give WordPerfect an Exit command.
2. When the screen shows

Save Document? (Y/N) Y

    press Enter to select Y (Yes).
3. When the screen shows

Document to be Saved: B:\ PHONE.LST

    press Enter again.
4. WordPerfect then asks if you're sure you want to replace the document on the disk with the one on the screen. It displays

Replace B:\ PHONE.LST? (Y/N) N

24

Type **y** to tell it Yes. The screen shows

Saving B: \ PHONE.LST

5. When

Exit WP? (Y/N) N

appears, press Enter to stay in WordPerfect.

Now WordPerfect clears the screen, at which point you may retrieve a new document from the disk. Suppose, however, you don't remember its name.

Finding Out What's on a Disk

To see what the data disk contains, press the F5 key to give WordPerfect a *List Files* command. When "Dir B: \ *.*" appears, press Enter. WordPerfect shows a list of available files at the top of the screen and the following list of options at the bottom:

1 Retrieve; 2 Delete; 3 Rename; 4 Print; 5 Text in;
6 Look; 7 Change Dir; 8 Copy; 9 Word Search: 0

At this point, you only have one file (PHONE.LST), but later you will have several. To retrieve the file that WordPerfect has highlighted, type 1; to retrieve another, press the arrow keys until its name is highlighted, then press 1. Thus, to retrieve the telephone list, highlight it and type 1.

Loading at Startup

If you know what file you want to work on (and remember its name), you can tell WordPerfect to load it when you start. To do this, enter **a:wp** and the filename when the B> prompt appears. For example, you could start WordPerfect with the telephone list by entering **a:wp phone.lst**.

EXITING WORDPERFECT

You should always use the Exit command to leave WordPerfect, rather than just turning the computer off. That is, press F7 to select *Exit*, save the current document (unless you have already done so or want to discard it), and then type **y** in response to the "Exit WP?" prompt. When the B> prompt appears, simply switch the power off if you are done.

Using the DOS Disk

To use the DOS disk, put it in the left-hand drive in place of the WordPerfect disk. Then type **a:** and Enter to activate that drive. At this point, the computer is waiting for you to enter a DOS command.

If you want to format a new disk, you will have to replace the data disk in the right-hand drive with the disk to be formatted. For the procedure to format a disk, refer to the WordPerfect Installation manual or to the FORMAT command in the IBM *DOS* manual.

Returning to WordPerfect

To leave DOS and return to WordPerfect, replace the DOS disk with the WordPerfect disk, type **b:** and Enter, then **a:wp** (or **a:wp** and a filename), and Enter again.

STARTING WORDPERFECT AFTER A POWER FAILURE

If you are using WordPerfect and absent-mindedly switch the computer off before doing an Exit operation, or the power goes off during an electrical storm, or someone accidentally dislodges the power cord, WordPerfect will not immediately work when you try to restart it. Instead, WordPerfect displays its copyright screen and shows the message *ERROR: Overflow File already exists* at the bottom. Shortly thereafter, the following option list appears:

Directory is in use! 1 Exit; 2 Use Another Directory;
3 Overwrite Files: 1

When this happens, type **3**. WordPerfect then deletes the files that are preventing you from starting and displays its normal starting screen.

DELETING DOCUMENTS

If you save a lot of work on disk, your data disks may end up containing some documents you no longer need. To discard or *delete* a document, press F5 to do a List Files command. When the list of files appears, move the highlighted bar to the file you want to delete and press **2** for *Delete*. Once you delete a file, it's lost forever. For this reason, WordPerfect asks

Delete B: \ filename? (Y/N) N

If you really want to proceed with the deletion, type **y**; otherwise, press Enter to get the menu back.

QUESTIONS AND ANSWERS

By now you probably have many questions, so let's stop and answer some.

Question: How can I make something appear on a line all by itself?

Answer: Press Enter before and after typing it. It will then always have a line to itself.

Question: How can I recover if I delete something unintentionally?

Answer: You can get it back from memory, by pressing F1 (for Cancel), and then typing **1** (for Restore).

Question: Why is everything I type appearing as capital letters?

Answer: You probably pressed Caps Lock by accident. Check the bottom line to see if the Position indicator reads *POS* (rather than *Pos*). If so, press the Caps Lock key to turn the lock off.

Question: When I try to move the cursor, the computer puts a number on the screen. What's wrong?

Answer: You pressed Num Lock by accident. Check the bottom line to see whether *Pos* is flashing. If it is, press Num Lock to turn the lock off.

Question: Why does the text move when I move the cursor right?

Answer: You're using the space bar instead of the right-arrow key. The space bar enters a space in place of whatever is at the cursor position.

Question: I just typed "rum" instead of "run". How do I correct it?

Answer: Press Backspace, then **n**. Note that the Del key won't do the job, because the cursor is already to the right of "rum".

Question: Whenever I enter something, it erases what I had before. What's wrong?

Answer: You have WordPerfect in the Typeover mode (*Typeover* should appear on the bottom line). To put it back in the normal (insertion) mode, press Ins.

Question: When I pressed Alt and F4 to obtain Block mode, the cursor went flying to the right-hand edge of the screen, taking my text with it. What's wrong?

Answer: You pressed Alt and F6 by mistake. This is WordPerfect's Flush Right command, which aligns text with the right margin. To retrieve the cursor and text, press the Backspace key. When *Delete [Aln/FlshR]? (Y/N) N* appears, type **y**.

HINTS AND WARNINGS

Always be aware of the following features of WordPerfect:

1. When you just type characters without pressing Ins, the characters you enter will be added to the text; they will not replace old characters.
2. Remember to use Backspace, not Del, to delete what you just typed.
3. If you have put WordPerfect in the Typeover mode, remember to return it to insert mode by pressing Ins after you finish replacing text. Other than showing *Typeover* on the status line, WordPerfect does not indicate that you are overtyping. Hence, it is easy to write over text you meant to keep.
4. When WordPerfect is in the Block mode, pressing Del and then y deletes all highlighted characters. Look before you leap, but remember that you can always leap backward with F1 (Cancel).
5. Do not leave a large amount of work in a vulnerable state. The power could go off, someone could trip over or dislodge the power cord, or you could accidentally turn the PC off without saving the text on disk. Always save your work every ten minutes or so. Remember to occasionally ask yourself whether you would like to reenter the material that is only in memory; if the answer is no, stop and save your work on disk.
6. Always give your disk documents reasonable names that suggest what they contain. It is difficult to remember what "D1" or "X" contains, but not what "FINRPT86" or "RESUME" means.

     Further, if your data disk is to store a variety of different documents, give them extensions that suggest their contents. For example, you could name letters with *.let*, lists with *.lst*, and reports with *.rpt*.
7. If you want to retrieve a document, but forget its name, press F5. WordPerfect will list the disk's filenames at the top of the screen and shade the first one. To retrieve that file, type 1; to retrieve any other, press the arrow keys until its name is shaded, and then type 1.
8. Always use the Exit (F7) command to exit WordPerfect or start working on a different document. WordPerfect will remind you to save your work before quitting. Unless there is a fire, resist the temptation to merely turn the computer off.

KEY POINT SUMMARY

Following are the key points you learned in this chapter. Table 2-1 summarizes the keys that were introduced.

1. WordPerfect keeps track of the length of text lines and starts a new line automatically when necessary. You should press Enter only when you reach the end of a paragraph or want to skip a line.
2. You can move the cursor by pressing keys on the numeric keypad. An arrow key moves the cursor in the direction it points. Holding it down keeps the

Table 2-1. Keys Introduced in Chapter 2.

Key(s)	Function
F1, 1	Restore deleted text
Alt-F4	Block mode
F5	List files on data disk
F7	Exit
Shift-F7	Print
F10	Save
Shift-F10	Retrieve
Backspace	Delete previous character
Ctrl-Backspace	Delete to end of word
Ctrl-End	Delete to end of line
Del	|*In insert, mode:*| Delete character
	|*In Block, mode:*| Delete block
Enter	|*In insert, mode:*| Start new paragraph
	|*In Block, mode:*| Select rest of paragraph
Ins	Typeover

Cursor-Moving Keys

Key(s)	Function
–	Top of screen
+	Bottom of screen
Left-arrow	Previous character
Right-arrow	Next character
Ctrl-Left-arrow	Previous word
Ctrl-Right-arrow	Next word
Up-arrow	Previous line
Down-arrow	Next line
Home, Home, Left-arrow	Beginning of line
End	End of line
Ctrl-Home, Character	Go to character

cursor moving in that direction. Pressing the - or + key moves the cursor to the beginning or end of the screen; pressing Home twice and then left-arrow, moves the cursor to the beginning of the line; pressing End moves it to the end of the line. WordPerfect always indicates the cursor's current line and column position on the status line at the top of the screen.

3. To move the cursor a word at a time, press Ctrl and either left-arrow (word left) or right-arrow (word right).

4. To move the cursor to a particular character, press Ctrl and Home (to give a Go To command), and then type the character. For example, to move it to the next paragraph, press Ctrl-Home and then Enter; to move it to the end of a sentence, press Ctrl-Home, and then type a period.

5. To insert text, move the cursor just to the right of where you want it to start, and then enter it.

6. To delete text, move the cursor to the first character, and then do one of the following things:

   - To delete the character at the cursor position, press Del.
   - To delete the previous character, press Backspace.
   - To delete to the end of the word, press Ctrl and Backspace.
   - To delete to the end of the line, press Ctrl and End.

7. You can also delete text in the Block mode. To do this, press Alt and F4 to select Block mode, move the cursor until WordPerfect highlights everything you want to delete, and then press Del. In Block mode, WordPerfect also lets you type the end character. For example, you can press Enter to select the rest of a paragraph or type a period (or other punctuation mark) to select the rest of a sentence or clause.

8. Whenever you delete something, WordPerfect temporarily saves it in the computer's memory. To copy deleted text back into a document, move the cursor to where you want it to appear, press F1, and then type 1.

9. To replace text, move the cursor to where the replacement should start, and press Ins (Insert) to put WordPerfect in the Typeover mode; then type the new material, and press Ins again to return to the insert mode.

10. To print a document, press Shift and F7, then type 1 to select *Full Text* or 2 to select *Page*.

11. There are two ways to save a document on the data disk: to continue working on the document, press F10 for Save; to start a new document, press F7 for Exit. When WordPerfect asks for the document name, enter it (up to eight characters, a period, and a three-character extension) and press Enter.

12. To load a document from disk, press Shift and F10 for Retrieve, enter the name, and press Enter.

    You can also load a document when you start WordPerfect. When the B> prompt appears, type **a:wp** and the document's name (e.g., type **a:wp phone.lst**), then press Enter.

13. To leave WordPerfect, press F7 for Exit.

14. To delete a document, give a List Files command; then select the file to be deleted and press **2**.

Chapter 3

Formal Correspondence

This chapter describes how to use WordPerfect to prepare formal business correspondence, such as requests for payment, order confirmations, and memoranda. Such correspondence usually has strict, standardized formats with precise margins and other special requirements. Furthermore, formal correspondence is often several pages long and may include repetitive names, addresses, or phrases.

Before entering a letter, you must restart WordPerfect. As before, put the WordPerfect disk in drive A and a data disk in drive B, and then turn the power on. The first thing the computer does is ask you for the date. Type it (e.g., type **7-20-86**); then press Enter. When the computer asks for the time, type it (e.g., type **9:30**) and press Enter again. Finally, type **b:** and Enter. When B> appears, type **a:wp** and Enter again. This makes WordPerfect display its basic blank screen.

SETTING TABS

Figure 3-1 shows a typical one-page business letter. Note that the return address, complimentary close, and the writer's name all start at the center of the page. The easiest way to place this material is to use a tab.

WordPerfect provides tabs at every fifth column (5, 10, 15, etc.). We want to clear these built-in tabs and fix a new one at the center of the line. WordPerfect's line extends from column 10 to column 74, so the center is at column 42.

To clear the tabs, press Shift and F8. When the following list appears

```
                            211 Washington Street
                            San Diego, CA 92121
                            July 3, 1986

Mr. Samuel Thompson
Gospel Island Computer Co.
146 Moonrise Drive
Inverness, FL 32650

Dear Mr. Thompson:

As of the close of business on 30 June 1986, your company has
outstanding invoices over 30 days old totaling $7,350.00.  We
must request immediate payment of these invoices or we will be
forced to add a 1 1/2% monthly service charge.

Until we receive payment, we cannot extend credit to your company
or process further orders.  Please remit this payment to my
attention as soon as possible.

                            Sincerely yours,



                            Marie F. Gerard
                            Assistant Credit Manager
```

Fig. 3-1. A business letter.

1 Tabs; 2 E-Tabs; 3 Margins; 4 Spacing; 5 Hyphenation;
6 Align Char: 0

type 1 for *Tabs*. WordPerfect displays two lines of dots, with a *T* at each column position that has a tab. To delete the tabs, press Ctrl and End. To fix a tab at column 42, type **42**, then Enter. Finally, to leave the tab setting area and return to the main screen, press F7 (Exit).

ENTERING THE BUSINESS LETTER

Now that you have set the tab, you can enter the letter from Fig. 3-1. Press the Tab key before typing the return address, since it must start at the center. Press Tab to reach the place where the date belongs. With WordPerfect, however, you need not enter the date (provided you entered it when you started the computer); you can tell WordPerfect to insert it!

Inserting the Date

To insert the date, press Shift and F5 to give a Date command. When Word-Perfect displays

Date 1 Insert Text; 2 Format; 3 Insert Function: 0

type 1 for *Insert Text*. This produces the date in the standard month-day-year format (e.g., *September 26, 1986*). Other formats are also available; see the Word-Perfect manual for details.

Finally, enter the body of the letter normally, but press Tab before typing **Sincerely yours,** and the writer's name and title. Remember to add an Extra Enter to skip a line.

SAVING AND PRINTING THE LETTER

To save the completed letter on disk, perform a *Save* command. That is, press F10, then enter **thompson** for the document name and press Enter. To print the letter, switch your printer *on-line,* then press Shift and F7 for *Print* and **2** for *Page*.

PROPORTIONAL SPACING

WordPerfect lets you print documents with proportional spacing. With this feature, the printer gives each character the amount of space equal to its width. For example, it gives an i less space than an m. Of course, your printer must be able to produce proportional spacing; not all can. To get proportional spacing, press Ctrl and F8 to select *Print Format*. This makes a Print Format menu, as shown in Fig. 3-2, appear.

To switch to proportional spacing, type **1** to select *Pitch*, then type **13*** for Pitch, and **3** and Enter for *Font*. Finally, press Enter once more to leave the Print Format menu. After that, when you print the document (by pressing Shift-F7 and then **2**), the printer will produce text that is proportionally-spaced as well as justified.

Figure 3-3 shows how our sample business letter would look if you printed it with the proportional spacing option.

TURNING JUSTIFICATION OFF

If you prefer to have your letters printed with a ragged-right margin instead of justified, simply turn off the justification. To do this, move the cursor to the

---

Print Format

1 -	Pitch	10
	Font	1
2 -	Lines per inch	6
	Right Justification	On
3 -	Turn off	
4 -	Turn on	
	Underline Style	5
5 -	Non-continuous Single	
6 -	Non-continuous Double	
7 -	Continuous Single	
8 -	Continuous Double	
9 -	Sheet Feeder Bin Number	1
A -	Insert Printer Command	

Selection: 0

Fig. 3-2. The print Format menu.

beginning of your document (or to any other place you want justification to stop), and then press Ctrl and F8 to obtain the Print Format menu. When it appears, type **3** to select *Turn off*, and then press Enter to return to editing. (You may also have to correct the Pitch and Font settings, if you changed them earlier.) Now, when you print the letter, it will appear just as it does on the screen.

MULTIPAGE LETTERS

So far, we have prepared only one-page letters. Formal correspondence, however, is often longer—sometimes *much* longer. For example, Fig. 3-4 shows a two-page memorandum summarizing a company's regional sales for the second quarter of 1986.

To enter this memorandum, create a new document. When WordPerfect's blank screen appears, enter the first page. After typing the final word Enclosure, press Enter.

Starting a New Page

To start a new page, give WordPerfect a Hard Page command by pressing Ctrl and Enter. When you do this, WordPerfect shows a dashed page-break line on the screen and moves the cursor below it. The status line message

Doc 1   Pg 2   Ln 1

indicates that the cursor is now at the top of a new page.

Setting Tabs for a Table

Before entering the sales table, we should set tabs for it. First, we must decide where the tabs go. The easiest way to do this is to enter the table headings

---

211 Washington Street
San Diego, CA 92121
July 3, 1986

Mr. Samuel Thompson
Gospel Island Computer Co.
146 Moonrise Drive
Inverness, FL 32650

Dear Mr. Thompson:

As of the close of business on 30 June 1986, your company has outstanding invoices over 30 days old totaling $7,350.00. We must request immediate payment of these invoices or we will be forced to add a 1 1/2% monthly service charge.

Until we receive payment, we cannot extend credit to your company or process further orders. Please remit this payment to my attention as soon as possible.

Sincerely yours,

Marie F. Gerard
Assistant Credit Manager

Fig. 3-3. A letter with proportional spacing.

This material is on the first page:

Date: July 15, 1986

To: Gloria A. Powell, National Sales Manager

From: Frank P. Hall, Southeast Regional Sales Manager

Subject: Second Quarter Sales

Attached are the second quarter sales figures for my region. As you can see, Cynthia Chamber continues to lead, but Jerry Leonard is gaining ground on her. Dick Morris is still at the bottom of the list; he blames that on the recent cancellation by the Wilson & Sons account.

In all, second quarter sales are 15 percent higher than those of last quarter.

Enclosure

This material is on the second page:

Southeast Region Sales, Second Quarter, 1986

State	Sales Rep.	Units Sold	Revenues ($)
Alabama	Adams, Jason	500	215,000
N. Carolina	Holmes, James	550	236,500
S. Carolina	Jackson, Charles	490	210,700
Florida	Chamber, Cynthia	640	275,200
Georgia	Grogan, Phyllis	420	180,600
Louisiana	Leonard, Jerome	610	262,300
Mississippi	Morris, Richard	320	137,600
Tennessee	Baker, Thomas	540	232,200
Virginia	Nelson, Patricia	480	206,400
Totals		4,550	1,956,500

Fig. 3-4. A two-page memorandum.

and the longest line of data (the *S. Carolina* line, in this case), then adjust the spacing. We can then see where to put the tabs.

To begin, enter the headings as follows, with three spaces between columns:

```
State   Sales Rep.   Units Sold   Revenues ($)
```

When you finish, press Enter twice to reach the line where the data starts. Then enter the *S. Carolina* line:

```
S. Carolina   Jackson, Charles   490   210,700
```

Now that we have entered the headings and the longest data line, we must adjust the spacing. To begin, move the cursor to the S in Sales, then press the space bar until the S is directly over the J in Jackson. Now move the cursor to the U in Units Sold and align it with the 4 in 490; this puts three spaces between the sales representative's name and the *Units Sold* heading.

Next we must center the last two data columns underneath their headings. To do this, put the cursor on the 4 in 490 and align it with the t in Units. Finally, put the cursor on the 2 in 210,700 and align it with the v in Revenues. When you are done, the screen should show:

```
State          Sales Rep.          Units Sold          Revenues ($)
S. Carolina    Jackson, Charles      490                 210,700
```

The tabs belong at the left edges of the data columns. To find out where these columns start, move the cursor to the data line and then towards the right to the beginning of each column. Note what *Pos* value appears on the status line each time; it tells you where to set the tab. If you have followed directions, you should find that the data columns start at columns 24, 46, and 58, respectively.

To set the tabs, press Shift and F8 to do a *Line Format* command, and then type 1 to select Tabs. As before, press Ctrl and End to clear the automatic tabs, then type **24** and Enter, **46** and Enter, and **58** and Enter. Now that the tabs have been set, press F7 to get back to editing.

You should now have tabs at columns 24, 46, and 58. To ensure that they are correct, move the cursor to the next line and press Tab three times, checking the *Pos* value each time. If, by chance, you have misplaced a tab, do another *Line Format* command (Shift-F8) and select *Tabs*. Then move the cursor to the incorrect Tab position and clear it by pressing Del. Finally, move the cursor to where this tab belongs and press Tab. When you finish setting tabs, press F7 to return to editing.

Completing the Table

The table contains eight more lines—two above the one you entered and six below it. To make room for the first two lines, move the cursor to the beginning of the *S. Carolina* line, then press Enter.

Enter the *Alabama* columns using Tab to move the cursor; press Enter at the end of the line. Enter the *N. Carolina* line in the same way. Now move the cursor to the blank line following the table and enter the remaining six data lines. When you finish, save the memorandum on disk by pressing F10. Name the memorandum salesq2.doc.

PAGING

In the preceding memorandum, we knew exactly where to end the first page and begin the second. However, we usually don't know ahead of time where page breaks will occur.

If you are using standard 11-inch paper, one page can hold 54 single-spaced lines. Thus, when you reach line 55, WordPerfect displays a dashed line across the screen and moves the cursor below it, to the top of a new page.

Keeping Paragraphs Together

Sometimes you may want to keep a paragraph all on one page. For example, the paragraph might contain a reference to a figure or table on the page.

To keep a paragraph together, give WordPerfect a Conditional Page Break command. This tells it "If the current page has fewer lines than the number I specify, start a new page." To begin a conditional page break, move the cursor to the line above the paragraph and press Alt and F8. This produces a Page Format menu (see Fig. 3-5). Type **9** to select "Conditional End of Page".

When the screen shows

> Number of lines to keep together =

enter the number of lines in the paragraph and press Enter once to return to the Page Format menu and then again to return to editing.

Preventing Widow and Orphan Lines

A possible disadvantage of automatic paging is that WordPerfect doesn't care how it arranges the text; it simply fills each page to capacity. Unlike a good typist, it may leave the first line of a paragraph alone at the bottom of a page (a *widow*) or leave the last line at the top of a new page (an *orphan*). Fortunately, you can break it of this sloppy habit.

```
Page Format
    1 - Page Number Position
    2 - New Page Number
    3 - Center Page Top to Bottom
    4 - Page Length
    5 - Top Margin
    6 - Headers or Footers
    7 - Page Number Column Positions
    8 - Suppress for Current page only
    9 - Conditional End of Page
    A - Widow/Orphan
Selection:  0
```

Fig. 3-5. The Page Format menu.

To make WordPerfect keep the first and last two lines of a paragraph with the rest of the paragraph on a page, do the following:

1. Put the cursor at the beginning of your document; then press Alt and F8 to obtain the Page Format menu.
2. When the Page Format menu appears, type **a** for "Widow/Orphan".
3. When WordPerfect shows *Widow/Orphan Protect (Y/N): N*, type **y** (for yes).
4. Press Enter to return to editing.

Keeping Tables Together

Because you press Enter at the end of each line in a table, WordPerfect will treat the lines as individual paragraphs and will split the table if it crosses a page break. To keep a table together, you can select the table as a block and then tell WordPerfect to *protect* the block: Do this as follows:

1. Move the cursor to the beginning of the table; then press Alt and F4 to put WordPerfect in Block mode.
2. When "Block on" appears at the bottom of the screen, move the cursor to the end of the table and press Alt and F8.
3. When WordPerfect asks *Block Protect? (Y/N) N*, type **y** for yes.

WordPerfect will then always keep the table on one page.

MOVING BETWEEN PAGES

Sometimes changes or corrections on one page will require changes on another page; or you may suddenly think of an error or omission on some other page. WordPerfect lets you move quickly to any page in a document.

Moving is simplest if the other page is the next one up or down from where you are working. Then all you do is press PgUp to move it back a page or PgDn to move it ahead a page. If the cursor is on the first or last line of a page, press the up-arrow key or down-arrow key to move it back a page or ahead a page, respectively.

To move to some other page, press Ctrl and Home. WordPerfect will display *Go to* at the bottom of the screen. Type the number of the page you want to work on and then press Enter. If, for example, you are working on page 4 and want to move to page 2, press Ctrl-Home, then type **2** and Enter. The computer will show *Repositioning* at the bottom of the screen and then display page 2 with the cursor at the top left-hand corner.

Further, you can move to the first or last page in a document without entering its page number. Just press Home twice and then either up-arrow (for the first page) or down-arrow (for the last page).

UNDERLINING

Writers use underlining for emphasis or to indicate a new term, a book title, or a magazine name. You can also use it to create mathematical symbols such as > or +.

To underline material, put the cursor at the start of it, press Alt and F4 to put WordPerfect in Block mode, extend the highlighting to cover the text to be underlined, then press the F8 (Underline) key. Remember, you can select a word with Ctrl and right-arrow, a line with End, a sentence by typing the end mark, or a paragraph by pressing Enter. For example, if your sales letter says

We must reduce the inventories of bedspreads this month.

you may want to underline *must* for emphasis. To do this, move the cursor to m, then press Alt-F4 (for Block mode), right-arrow four times (to extend the highlighting), and F8. Pressing F8 here takes WordPerfect out of Block mode.

You can also make WordPerfect underline material as you type it. When you get to where the underlining should begin, press F8. After that, WordPerfect will underline everything—even spaces—until you press F8 again. For example, suppose you want to enter

Our company's name is Frank O. Gold, Inc., not Franco Goldink, as in your recent article.

To produce it, you would type normally up the F in Frank and press F8. Type Frank O. Gold, Inc. (WordPerfect underlines it), press F8 again, and finish the sentence.

Note, incidentally, that while underlining is active, WordPerfect underlines the *Pos* value at the bottom right-hand corner of the screen.

Removing Underlining

You can also remove underlining, by deleting WordPerfect's invisible underline code. To do this, move the cursor to where the underlining starts, then press the Alt and F3 to give WordPerfect a Reveal Codes command. When you do this, WordPerfect leaves only seven lines of text at the top of the screen: the line the cursor is on and the three lines above and below it. Below the text is a lighted bar, followed by the text filled with strange codes in brackets.

The lighted bar is called the *Tab Ruler*. It marks the current tab positions with triangles, the left-hand margin with a [symbol, and the right-hand margin with a] symbol.

The codes are internal commands to WordPerfect. For example, [SRt] (for Soft Return) tells it to start a new line, while [HRt] (for Hard Return) marks where you pressed Enter; it tells WordPerfect to start a new paragraph. The blinking [^] indicates the current cursor position. (Note that the cursor is still displayed in the regular text as well.)

If you put the cursor on the first underlined character, the cursor indicator is preceded by [U]. This marks the start of underlining (a [u] marks the end). To remove underlining, delete the [U] by pressing the Backspace key. Note that Backspace removes underlining from both the Reveal Codes text and the regular text at the top. Now you can press Enter to return to your document.

CENTERING

Tables usually require centered titles. You can produce one by pressing Shift and F6, or you can center an existing title by putting the cursor on the first character and then pressing Shift-F6.

Let's center the title on page 2 of the memorandum in Fig. 3-4. Load salesq2.doc into the computer from disk using the Retrieve option. Move the cursor to page 2 by pressing PgDn, and then move it to the beginning of the title. Center the title by pressing Shift and F6. Finally, press F10 to save the memorandum with the centered title.

Uncentering

Just as WordPerfect uses an invisible code to turn underlining on, it uses another code to produce centering. Thus, to uncenter a line, put the cursor at the start of it and use a Reveal Codes command to delete the centering code ([C]).

NUMBERING PAGES

If your letter is longer than two pages, you may want to number the pages. To begin, move the cursor to the beginning of the document or the page where you want numbering to start (say, you want it to start on the second page). Now, press Alt and F8 to obtain the Page Format menu; then press 1 for *Page Number Position*. This produces a menu that lets you choose where page numbers should appear. The options are:

- No page numbers (the default setting)
- Top left corner of every page
- Top center of every page
- Top right corner of every page
- Top, alternating left and right corner
- Bottom left corner of every page
- Bottom center of every page
- Bottom right corner of every page
- Bottom, alternating left and right corner

Type the number of the position you want, and then press Enter to leave the menu. You won't see page numbers on the screen, but they will appear in your document when you print it.

Page Numbers in Text

You can also refer to the current page number within your text. When you get to where you want WordPerfect to insert the page number, press Ctrl and B; the screen shows ^B. When you print the document, WordPerfect will replace ^B with the page number.

QUESTIONS AND ANSWERS

Question: I keep reaching for the Tab key and nothing happens. What's the problem?

Answer: Look where you're reaching. You're probably pressing Ctrl instead of Tab.

Question: How can I force WordPerfect to start a new page?

Answer: Put the cursor at the end of the current page and press the Ctrl and Enter keys. This gives WordPerfect a Hard Page command.

Question: How can I make sure that WordPerfect doesn't split a table between two pages?

Answer: Move the cursor to the beginning of the table and press Alt and F4 to put WordPerfect in Block mode. Then move the cursor to the end of the table and press Alt and F8. When the screen shows *Protect Block? (Y/N) N*, type y.

Question: While working on page 7 of a long letter, I decided to change some terms that I mentioned on page 2. How do I get back and forth?

Answer: Give WordPerfect a Go to command by pressing Ctrl and Home; then type 2 and Enter. Make your changes and press Ctrl-Home twice (you needn't enter a page number either time) to return to page 7. If page 7 is as far as you have typed, you can press Home twice and then the down-arrow to return to it.

Question: I only want to underline words, not the spaces between them. How can I do this?

Answer: You must underline each word individually. If you haven't yet typed the words, press F8 before and after each one. If they're already in your document, move to the first one, press Alt and F4 to put WordPerfect in Block mode, press the right-arrow key until the word is highlighted, and then press F8. Do the same thing for the rest of the words you underlined.

Question: I underlined a word in my letter, but forgot to turn underlining off at the end of it, so WordPerfect underlined the next word as well. How can I fix this?

Answer: Move the cursor to the start of the underlining, and then use the Reveal Codes command to delete the [U] code. This removes the underlining from both words. To underline the first word, select it in Block mode and press F8 to underline it.

Question: I meant to press Ctrl and Home to change pages, but instead I pressed Ctrl and Enter, and WordPerfect inserted a Hard Page break. How can I delete the break?

Answer: Move the cursor to the end of the line that precedes the break, and then press Del.

HINTS AND WARNINGS

1. WordPerfect automatically provides tabs at every fifth column position. To change the tabs, press Shift and F8 to obtain the Line Format menu, then type 1 to select *Tabs*. To clear all of the tabs, press Ctrl and End. To clear a particular tab, move to it and press Del. To add a new tab, enter its column number. When you finish, press F7 to return to editing.

2. To switch from justified text to unjustified (ragged-right) text, or vice versa, you must start with the cursor where you want the change to begin. (This is generally at the beginning of the document.) If you change the Print Format menu midway through the document, part of it will print justified, while the rest will print ragged-right.

3. Both Block Protect and Conditional End of Page can be used to keep material on a page. However, Block Protect should be used to keep large blocks together, while Conditional End of Page is more suited to keeping smaller blocks together. Hence, you would use Block Protect to preserve a table or graph, and Conditional End of Page to preserve a short paragraph or keep a title with the first paragraph of text.

KEY POINT SUMMARY

Table 3-1 summarizes the keys that were introduced in this chapter.

1. WordPerfect automatically provides tabs at every fifth column position (5, 10, 15, etc.). To change them, press Shift and F8 for *Line Format*, then type

Table 3-1. Keys Introduced in Chapter 3.

Key(s)	Function
Alt-F3	Reveal Codes
Shift-F5	Date
Shift-F6	Center current line
F8	|*In edit mode:*| Turn underlining on or off
	|*In Block mode:*| Underline selected text
Alt-F8	|*In edit mode:*| Page Format
	|*In Block mode:*| Block protect
Ctrl-F8	Print Format
Shift-F8	Line Format
Ctrl-B	Page number
Ctrl-End	|*When changing tabs:*| Clear all tabs
Ctrl-Enter	Hard Page (start a new page)
Cursor-Moving Keys	
Ctrl-Home, page number	Specified page
Home, Home, Up-arrow	Beginning of text
Home, Home, Down-arrow	End of text
PgUp	Preceding page
PgDn	Next page

1 for *Tabs*. When the tabs form appears, you may set a new tab by entering its column number, clear all tabs by press Ctrl and End, or delete a particular tab by moving to it and pressing Del. Finally, press F7 to return to editing.

2. To insert the current date in a document, press Shift and F5 to select *Date*, and then type **1** to make the insertion.

3. WordPerfect's Print Format menu lets you specify parameters for printing. To obtain it, press Ctrl and F8. Once the menu appears you can order proportional spacing (type **1**; then type **10★** for Pitch and **3** for Font, and press Enter) or turn justification off (type **3**) or on (type **4**). To leave the menu, press Enter. Now you may print the document.

4. WordPerfect automatically divides single-spaced text into 54-line pages. You can, however, force it to start a new page anywhere by pressing Ctrl and Enter to give a Hard Page command.

5. You can force WordPerfect to keep a paragraph together by giving a Conditional Page Break command. To do this, move the cursor to the line that precedes the paragraph and press Alt and F8 to obtain the Page Format menu. When it appears, type **9** for *Conditional End of Page*, enter the line length of the paragraph, and press Enter twice.

6. By changing *Widow/Orphan Protect* to *Y* (for yes) from the Page Format menu, WordPerfect will no longer leave the first line or last line of a paragraph alone on a page.

7. To keep a table together on a page, select it in Block mode, and press Alt and F8 for *Block Protect*. When WordPerfect asks *Block Protect?*, type **y**.

8. To move the cursor to the previous page or the next page, press PgUp or PgDn. To move it to the beginning or end of the document, press Home twice and then either up-arrow (beginning) or down-arrow (end). To move it to any other page, press Ctrl and Home. In response to the prompt, enter a page number and press Enter.

9. To underline existing material, select it in Block mode, and press F8. To underline new material, press F8 to turn underlining on, type the material, and then press F8 again to turn underlining off.

10. To center an existing line, move the cursor to the start of it, and then press Shift and F6. To center a new line, press Shift-F6 before you type it.

11. To remove underlining or centering, move the cursor to the character where it starts, and press Alt and F3 for *Reveal Codes*. When the coded text appears, press Backspace to delete the code ([U] for underline or [C] for center) and Enter to get back to editing.

12. To make WordPerfect print page numbers on your document, move the cursor to where you want numbering to begin, press Alt-F8 to obtain the Page Format menu, type **1** for *Page Number Position,* and then select the position.

You can also make WordPerfect insert the current page number in text; simply press Ctrl and B where it is to appear.

Chapter 4

Speller and Thesaurus

WordPerfect includes a Speller and Thesaurus that can help improve the quality of your work. The *Speller* can check a document, or a portion of one, for spelling errors. It does this by looking for each word in its dictionary. If a word is not there, the Speller highlights it and displays a list of close words from the dictionary; you can then choose from the list. If the word you're after is not in the list, you can tell the Speller to skip it (e.g., it is a proper name or part of a book title), add it to a supplementary dictionary (e.g., it is a technical term not found in most dictionaries), correct it manually, or request a list of words that match the general pattern of or sound similar to, the misspelled word.

The Speller also marks duplicated words (as in "All the the students got good grades.") and provides a count of the words it checked.

The *Thesaurus* is similar to the popular book version, but it is much faster because the synonyms appear on the screen almost instantaneously. To obtain a list of synonyms, you simply move the cursor to the word in question and then start the Thesaurus. The Thesaurus displays a list of nouns, verbs, and adjectives appropriate to that word. You can then either choose a replacement from the list, temporarily return to the document, or display more synonyms.

STARTING THE SPELLER

WordPerfect can spell-check a word, a page, or an entire document. To check a word, move the cursor to the start of it; to check a page or document, put the cursor anywhere in it. To start the Speller, put the Speller disk in drive B (replacing the data disk), then press Ctrl and F2 to give WordPerfect a Spell command. This produces the following menu at the bottom of the screen:

Check: 1 Word; 2 Page; 3 Document; 4 Change Dictionary;
5 Look Up; 6 Count

Now, type **1**, **2**, or **3**. The Speller checks each word against its dictionary, and shows *Please Wait* during the checking operation.

If it can't find a word in the dictionary, it highlights the word and displays a list of close words (if any) in the middle of the screen and this menu at the bottom:

Not Found! Select Word or Menu Option (0 = Continue): 0
1 Skip Once; 2 Skip; 3 Add Word; 4 Edit; 5 Look Up; 6 Phonetic

At this point, you have two options. If the correct word appears in the list, simply type the letter that precedes it; otherwise, you can choose from the six options on the bottom line. Here is an explanation of these options:

- *1 - Skip Once*. This makes the Speller continue spell-checking, but tells it to stop at the next occurrence of the word (if any).
- *2 - Skip*. This lets you skip a word you don't use often enough to want to add to the dictionary.
- *3 - Add Word*. This makes the Speller create a supplementary dictionary (if it doesn't already exist) and add this word to it. In future spell-checking operations, the Speller will automatically search the extra dictionary as well as the standard one.
- *4 - Edit*. This lets you correct a word manually. When the Speller moves the cursor to the word, type the correct spelling and then press Enter.
- *5 - Look Up*. This lets you search the dictionary for words that have the same general form as the marked word. More about this option later.
- *6 - Phonetic*. This makes the Speller display words that sound like this one.

Options 2, 3, and 4 operate not only on the current word, but on every occurrence of that word throughout your document. That is, if you skip a word (2), the Speller will ignore subsequent occurrences it encounters. Similarly, if you change a word either from a list (3) or manually (4), the Speller will make the same correction to all later occurrences.

When the Speller has finished spell-checking, it shows a word count and *Press any key to continue* appears at the bottom of the screen. When this appears, remove the Speller disk from drive B and replace it with the data disk on which you want to save the corrected document. Then press Enter.

Duplicated Words

The Speller will also check for duplicated words, as in "I drove the the car." If it encounters them, it displays

Double Word!   1 2 Skip; 3 Delete 2nd; 4 Edit;
5 Disable double word checking

Here, you would normally type **3**, to delete the second word. But you can also type **1** or **2** to skip this occurrence (but not subsequent ones), **4** to edit (say, to insert a hyphen between the words), or **5** to ignore double words.

AN EXAMPLE OF SPELLING CORRECTION

As an example of using the Speller, consider the letter in Fig. 4-1. With the aid of *Webster's New World Misspeller's Dictionary*, a few typing mistakes, and our own ingenuity, we have introduced several spelling errors. If you try this example on your own, don't be restricted by our mistakes; surely you can make bigger, better, or different ones.

Once you have entered the letter, insert the Speller disk in drive B, then press Ctrl and F2 for *Spell*. When the Speller displays its Check menu, type **3** for document.

The program proceeds to search the document for words that it cannot find in its dictionary. Besides misspellings, these may include proper names, abbreviations, and technical terms. In our case, it finds ten unmatched words (starting with *rikwest* in the first paragraph), and puts the Not Found menu at the bottom of the screen each time.

Dealing With Unmatched Words

Here, we deal with the ten unmatched words by using the following:

- We typed **6** to search for words that sound like *rikwest, resullution,* and *burows*. In each case, the Speller produced a list of choices. For *rikwest*, for example, it showed

---

2211 Washington Street
San Diego, CA 92121
May 16, 1986

Mr. Carl Johnson
1236 Summit Drive
San Diego, CA 92121

Dear Mr. Johnson:

In response to your recent rikwest, we need the following
information to cunsider a credit applivdation:

    1) Name and adddress of your bank, along with your account
       number.
    2) Three credit references.
    3) A signed corprate resullution indicating trepponsabillity
       for payment.

You may either use our enclosed form or sumbit a standard one of
your own. Please indicate any ratings you may have from credit
burows.

                Sincerely yours,

                Marie F. Gerard
                Assistant Credit Manager

Enclosure

Fig. 4-1. A credit application letter with misspellings.

A. raciest	B. racist	C. reaccused
D. recast	E. recessed	F. recused
G. reqeust	H. request	I. requested
J. requisite	K. richest	L. rockiest
M. roughest		

    Here, we pressed **h** for *request*.
- The words *cunsider, adddress, corprate,* and *sumbit* were so close to those in
  the dictionary that the Speller was able to display the correct version. Hence,
  we typed the identifying letter to make the replacement.
- We typed **3** to add *Gerard* to a supplementary dictionary. (Surprisingly, the

Speller already had *San Diego, CA, Carl, Johnson, Marie,* and *F.* in its main dictionary!)

- We typed **4** to manually change *applivdation* to *application* and *trepponsabillity* to *responsabillity.* In the second case, however, the Speller marked *responsabillity* as still misspelled. But then, the Not Found menu's option 6 gave us the correct form, so we were home free.

SPELL-CHECKING A BLOCK OF TEXT

You can also spell-check a sentence, paragraph, or any other selected portion of a document. To do this, put the cursor where you want to start, and then press Alt and F4 to put WordPerfect into Block mode. Then move the cursor just past the last word you want to check (WordPerfect highlights everything in between) and press Ctrl and F2 to start the Speller.

LOOKING UP WORDS

Selecting option 5, *Look Up,* in either the main Check menu or the Not Found menu makes the Speller show the prompt

Word or Word Pattern:

In response, you may enter either a word or a word *pattern* (details are upcoming). If you enter a word, the Speller displays a list of words that sound the same as the one you entered. If you enter a pattern, the Speller displays a list of similarly spelled words.

Looking Up "Sound-Alikes"

If you enter a specific word in response to the *Word or Word Pattern* prompt, the Speller will produce a list of the words that sound like it; that is, *homonyms.* This is handy for finding the correct form of a word that for which you aren't reasonably sure of the spelling. For example, entering *reconsiliation* makes the Speller produce the correct *reconciliation,* while entering *iridesent* or *eradesent* makes it produce *iridescent*

Looking Up Word Patterns

You can also enter a word pattern in response to the *Word or Word Pattern* prompt. Within the pattern, you can insert two *wildcard* symbols as place markers for the letters you want the Speller to supply. Specifically, you can enter a question mark (?) to represent a single letter or an asterisk (*) to represent an unspecified number of consecutive letters.

The question mark is useful for finding out which vowel belongs in a word. For example, if you don't know whether *durable* is spelled *durable, dureble,* or *durible,* enter the pattern *dur?ble;* the Speller lists only *durable.* Similarly, the pattern *hom?ly* produces both *homely* and *homily;* choose the one you want.

Perhaps the best use of the asterisk is to indicate whether a particular word contains one or two occurrences of a letter. For example, if you're not sure how to spell *accommodate* (two c's and two m's, one c and two m's, etc.), enter *ac*m*date;* the Speller produces *accommodate.* Similarly, the pattern *rec*om*end* produces the correct form *recommend.* Note that * can represent any number of letters, or even no letters, whereas ? can only represent a single letter. Thus, if you enter *rec?om?end* (as per the preceding example), the Speller will not find the form you want.

The asterisk is also useful for finding the correct combination of two or more letters. For example, entering *finag** informs you that the correct form is *finagle* (rather than *finagel*) and entering *us*ble* produces *usable* (rather than *useable*).

Besides its use in everyday writing work, the Look Up option is also handy for less important tasks, such as solving crossword puzzles. Some examples are:

- Entering the pattern r?nt makes the Speller display all the four-letter words that start with r and end with nt—*rant, rent,* and *runt,* in this case.
- Entering ran?? makes it display all the three- to five-letter words that start with ran. This produces *ran, randy, range, ranks,* and so on.
- The similar form ran* makes it display all the words that start with ran, regardless of their length.
- Entering r*n makes it display words that start with r and end with n. This produces words as short as *ran* and as long as *radiosterilization.*

STARTING THE THESAURUS

WordPerfect's Thesaurus can look up synonyms for a word on the screen or for one you type after you begin to use the Thesaurus, and insert any synonym in the document. To begin, put the Thesaurus disk in drive B (replacing the data disk) and then move the cursor to the word you want to look up (or to where it belongs, if you haven't yet typed it). Finally, press Alt and F1 to give WordPerfect a Thesaurus command.

FINDING SYNONYMS FOR EXISTING WORDS

When you start the Thesaurus, it searches for the word at the cursor position and then does either of two things. If the Thesaurus does not contain that particular word, it displays the message *Not a headword* and the prompt *Word* at the bottom of the screen. Now you can either enter another word (if, say, it's misspelled on the screen) or press the F1 (*Cancel*) key twice to get back to your document.

If your word is a *headword* (a word for which the Thesaurus contains synonyms), the Thesaurus lists the synonyms—nouns, verbs, and adjectives—and puts the following menu at the bottom of the screen:

1 Replace Word; 2 View Doc; 3 Look Up Word; 4 Clear Column: 0

Your choices are as follows:

- *1 - Replace Word.* This makes the Thesaurus replace the word with one from the list. When you type **1**, the screen shows *Press letter for word.* Type the identifying letter of the synonym you want; the Thesaurus makes the replacement.
- *2 - View Doc.* This lets you temporarily leave the Thesaurus so you can display other parts of your text. Move through your document as you do during editing using the arrow keys, PgUp, PgDn, and so on. To return to the Thesaurus (and to the original place in your text), press F7, the Exit key.
- *3 - Look Up Word.* If a synonym in the list is close to what you want, and it is preceded by a bullet, use this option to obtain synonyms for the close word. The bullets indicate *headwords*—that is, words for which the Thesaurus contains synonyms.

  When you press **3**, *Word* and your word appears at the bottom of the screen. To obtain synonyms for a headword, simply type its identifying letter and press Enter. The Thesaurus displays them in the next available column, and moves the lettering to that column. The lettered column is the active one. To activate a different column, press the right-arrow or left-arrow key to select the next column or the preceding one.
- *4 - Clear Column.* This erases the active column and moves the lettering to the preceding column. It's handy if you have used option 3 and decide you don't want any of the synonyms it produced. Clearing the column opens up more screen space for a preceding set of synonyms.

FINDING SYNONYMS FOR NEW WORDS

You can also use the Thesaurus to suggest synonyms for a word you haven't yet entered into your document. To do this, put the cursor on the space where the new word should start, and then start the Thesaurus. When *Word:* appears at the bottom of the screen, enter the word you want to look up and press Enter. From here on, the operation proceeds just as it would with an existing word.

QUESTIONS AND ANSWERS

Question: I corrected the spelling in a four-page letter, but have since made changes to page 2. How can I correct just that page?

Answer: Move the cursor to page 2 and start the Speller as usual. When its menu appears, type **2** for *Page*.

Question: The Speller marked the name of my company as misspelled, so I added it to the dictionary. There are more mentions of the company in my letter. Do I have to correct as well?

Answer: No. Once you select a replacement from the dictionary (by typing its identifier letter or using option 6 in the Not Found menu), skip a word (option 2 in the Not Found menu), add it to the dictionary (option 3), or change the spelling from the keyboard (option 4), the Speller will change all subsequent occurrences of the word throughout your document.

HINTS AND WARNINGS

1. WordPerfect's Speller acts as a proofreader as well as a spelling checker. Many of the errors it finds are really typing mistakes.
2. Even if you are reasonably sure of a correction, you might as well have the Speller look it up. This takes only a few seconds and verifies the spelling.
3. In practice, you should add abbreviations, proper names, and technical terms to the dictionary rather than just ignoring them. If you skip them, the Speller will find them every time it spell-checks a document. This is time consuming and annoying.
4. The Speller will not locate double punctuation (e.g., ''Bill,, that's the best thing you ever said.''); nor will it detect missing spaces following a punctuation mark (e.g., ''This is the end;there is no more.''), as long as both words are valid. You must correct these yourself.
5. The Speller counts words as it spell-checks a document and displays the total when it finishes. This is handy for writers and students who want to prepare an article, short story, report, or term paper of a specific length.
6. The Speller's Look Up option is handy for finding correct spellings as you work. When you are about to type a word you aren't sure of, press Ctrl and F2 for *Spell*, then **5** for *Look Up*. Type your best guess of the word's spelling and press Enter. The Speller will display a list of all the words that sound like the one you entered.
7. To stop a spell-check operation before it finishes, press F1, the Cancel key.
8. the Thesaurus menu on the screen, you can return to your document by pressing Enter.

KEY POINT SUMMARY

Table 4-1 summarizes the keys we introduced in this chapter.

1. WordPerfect can spell-check a word, a page, or an entire document. To check

Table 4-1. Keys introduced in Chapter 4.

Keys	Function
Ctrl-F2	Speller
Alt-F1	Thesaurus

a word, move the cursor to the start of it; to check a page or document, put the cursor anywhere in it.

2. To start the Speller, put the Speller disk in drive B, then press Ctrl and F2 to give WordPerfect a Spell command. When the Check menu appears, type **1**, **2**, or **3** for Word, Page, or Document.

3. If the Speller can't find a word in its dictionary, it highlights the word and displays a list of close words (if any) in the middle of the screen and a Not Found menu at the bottom. If the correct word appears in the list, simply type the letter that precedes it; otherwise, choose from the six options on the bottom line.

4. The Not Found menu's options let you *Skip Once* and proceed to the next occurrence, *Skip* this word and all other occurrences, *Add Word* to a supplementary dictionary, *Edit* the word from the keyboard, *Look Up* words that have the same general pattern, or look up words that have the same *Phonetic* sound as this one.

5. The Not Found menu's *Look Up* option lets you enter a pattern for words you want to view. The pattern can include a ? to represent a single letter or an * to represent a series of consecutive letters.

6. When the Speller finishes, it shows a word count and *Press any key to continue* at the bottom of the screen. When this appears, replace the Speller disk with the document's data disk and press Enter.

7. WordPerfect's Thesaurus can look up synonyms for a word on the screen or one you haven't typed yet, and insert any synonym in the document. To begin, put the Thesaurus disk in drive B, then move the cursor to the word you want to look up (or to where it belongs, if you haven't yet typed it). Finally, press Alt and F1 to give a *Thesaurus* command.

8. If the Thesaurus does not contain the word you have requested, it displays *Not a headword*, then *Word* at the bottom of the screen. Now you can either enter another word or press the F1 *Cancel* key twice to get back to your document.

9. If your word is a valid headword, the Thesaurus lists the synonyms—nouns, verbs, and adjectives—and puts a menu at the bottom of the screen. The menu lets you *Replace Word* with one from the list, *View Doc* (move through your document, to see more context), *Look Up Word* (obtain other synonyms for a listed headword), or *Clear Column* to erase the active column and move the lettering to the preceding column.

10. To find synonyms for a word you haven't yet entered into your document, put the cursor on the space where the new word should start and then start the Thesaurus. When *Word:* appears at the bottom of the screen, type the word you want to look up and press Enter. From here on, the operation proceeds just as it would with an existing word.

Chapter 5

Reports

To write a report with WordPerfect, you will need features we have not yet discussed. For example, you will want the pages numbered. You may also want a heading on the top of each page and the chapter number, section title, or report title at the bottom.

Furthermore, you may want the report double-spaced, but with single-spaced lists or tables. You may also want titles in **bold** print, and you may want to use subscripts or superscripts in references, equations, and formulas.

SAMPLE REPORT

Figures 5-1A through 5-1E show a sample five-page report concerning a company's quarterly sales. It consists of a cover page, followed by three summary tables and accompanying descriptions. Note the following:

- All titles are in bold print.
- Descriptive text is double-spaced and has a ragged right-hand margin.
- Tables are centered.
- The page number and report title appear at the bottom of every page except the cover.

We will enter this report and discuss its features as we encounter them. To begin, start WordPerfect as usual.

```
                    ACME CORPORATION

                  National Sales Report

                  Second Quarter, 1986
```

```
Gloria A. Powell
National Sales Manager
July 19, 1986

cc: P.M. Cornell, President
    J.R. Johnson, Vice-President
    Regional Sales Managers
```

Fig. 5-1A. Sample report, cover page.

This report summarizes national sales for the second quarter of 1986. Table 1 lists the sales figures for the six regions and compares them to the second quarter of 1985. As the table shows, sales are moderately better than last year in every region except the Southwest.

The Southeast region tops the list with a 9.9 percent gain, due in part to large orders from Jenco in Florida and Symtech in Georgia. Although the Southwest region continues to lead in volume, its sales are slightly below last year's. This reflects decreased orders from Winicon Corp. in Nevada, which has been troubled by economic conditions. In all, this quarter's sales are <u>5.7 percent higher</u> than those of the second quarter of 1984.

Table 2 lists the leading sales representatives in each region. These are the same people listed on last year's report, with one exception: Doris Kim, who joined Acme in January, closed a 290-unit order with Pacifico to put her on top in the Northwest. Our sales force continues to be among the best in the business, but I am especially proud of the exceptional individuals listed here.

-2- (Second Quarter Report/1986)

Fig. 5-1B. Sample report, second page.

Table 1. Second Quarter Sales

Region	Units Sold	Revenues ($)	% Change from 1985
Northeast	5,770	2,481,100	+6.7
Southeast	4,550	1,956,500	+9.9
Midwest	6,430	2,764,900	+8.8
Mountain	4,300	1,849,000	+4.7
Northwest	5,130	2,205,900	+7.4
Southwest	6,780	2,915,400	-0.3
Totals	32,960	14,172,800	+5.7

Table 2. Top Sales Representatives

Region	Sales Rep.	Units Sold	% Increase from 1985
Northeast	R. Roberts	790	22.4
Southeast	C. Chamber	640	16.3
Midwest	J. Wilkes	730	19.1
Mountain	P. Wallach	620	20.6
Northwest	D. Kim	590	--
Southwest	B. Lloyd	710	17.7

Fig. 5-1C. Sample report, third page.

Table 3 lists the orders that were placed by key accounts during the quarter. Most significant of these is the 510-unit order by Chicago Gear, whose orders appeared to have leveled off at about 400 units per quarter during the past two years. The Wilburg Sons and Storr Brothers accounts also show notable increases; both orders are about 19 percent higher than in recent quarters.

-4- (Second Quarter Report/1986)

Fig. 5-1D. Sample report, fourth page.

Table 3. Orders by Key Accounts

Region	Account	State	Sales Rep.	Order
Northeast	Wilburg Sons	New York	R. Roberts	430
Southeast	Jenco	Florida	C. Chamber	390
	Symtech	Georgia	P. Grogan	240
Midwest	Chicago Gear	Illinois	J. Wilkes	510
Mountain	Hart Foods	Montana	P. Wallach	420
Northwest	Pacifico	Oregon	D. Kim	290
Southwest	Storr Bros.	California	B. Lloyd	470

Fig. 5-1E. Sample report, fifth page.

ENTERING THE COVER PAGE

As Fig. 5-1A shows, the cover has a centered, bold title and the author's name and title, the date, and the distribution list (''cc'' means carbon copy) in the lower left-hand corner. In this figure, the title starts three inches from the top.

Although WordPerfect automatically provides a one-inch top margin, you must still move the cursor two inches down the page. To do this, press Enter 12 times (WordPerfect's default spacing is six lines per inch), then press Shift and F6 to prepare WordPerfect for centering.

Bold Print

To make something print in **bold** type, press F6. WordPerfect emboldens the *Pos* value at the bottom right-hand corner of the screen. This means it will embolden everything you type until you press F6 again. (This can be a character, word, paragraph, or even an entire document.)

Finishing the Cover Page

To embolden the title on the cover page, do the following:

1. Press F6 to turn emboldening on.
2. Type **ACME CORPORATION** and press Enter twice.
3. Press Shift and F6, then type **National Sales Report** and press Enter twice.
4. Press Shift and F6; then type **Second Quarter, 1986** and press F6 (to turn emboldening off) and Enter.

To complete the page, you must press Enter to reach the line where the author's name goes. Since we want seven lines (including a blank line) at the bottom of a 54-line page, the author's name belongs on line 48. Hence, press Enter until the status line at the bottom shows *Ln 48*. Then enter the author's name and title, the date, and the distribution list.

Pressing Enter after you type **Regional Sales Managers** moves the cursor to the top of the second page.

ENTERING THE SECOND PAGE

The second page has two features we have not used before; it is double-spaced and has a page number at the bottom.

DOUBLE SPACING

To double space the second page, you must change the Spacing value using WordPerfect's Line Format menu. To begin, press Shift and F8 to obtain the menu, then type **4** for *Spacing*. WordPerfect shows

[Spacing Set] 1

at the bottom of the screen. The *1* means that WordPerfect is currently set for single spacing. To switch to double spacing, type **2** press Enter. Now WordPerfect will both display and print double spaced text.

HEADERS AND FOOTERS

Let us now make WordPerfect print the following line at the bottom of pages 2 through 5.

-n- (Second Quarter Report/1986)

where n is the page number. The WordPerfect manual calls text that appears at the bottom of every page a *footer*. You can also make text appear at the top of every page, as a *header*.

When you create a header or footer, you must tell WordPerfect where and when to print it. You can specify up to two headers and two footers. For example, you can have a section title at the top of right-hand (odd-numbered) pages, the report title at the top of left-hand (even-numbered) pages, and the page number at the bottom of every page.

Creating a Header or Footer

To create a header or footer, move the cursor to the top of the first page where you want one, and press Alt-F8 to obtain the Page Format menu. When it appears, type **6** to select *Headers or Footers* to obtain the Header/Footer Specification menu (see Fig. 5-2).

Header/Footer Specification

Type	**Occurrence**
1 - Header A	0 - Discontinue
2 - Header B	1 - Every Page
3 - Footer A	2 - Odd Pages
4 - Footer B	3 - Even Pages
	4 - Edit
Selection: 0	Selection: 0

Fig. 5-2. The Header/Footer Specification menu.

Now proceed as follows:

1. Select the *Type* you want, Header A or B or Footer A or B. (*A* is the first header or footer, while *B* is the second.)
2. Select the *Occurrence*. This can be *Discontinue* (to omit a previously-defined header or footer), *Every Page,Odd Pages, Even Pages,* or *Edit* (to change an existing header or footer). WordPerfect then clears the screen and shows *Press EXIT when done* at the bottom.
3. Enter the text for the header or footer just as you would enter regular text. You can center or underline it using standard methods.

    To make WordPerfect print the page number in a header or footer, press Ctrl and B where you want it to appear. The screen shows ^B there.
4. Press F7, the *Exit* key, to return to the Page Format menu; then press Enter to return to your document.

The Footer for the Sample Report

To enter the footer for the sample report, do the following:

1. Press Alt-F8 to obtain the Page Format menu.
2. Type **6** to select *Headers or Footers*. WordPerfect displays the Header/Footer Specification menu.
3. To tell WordPerfect where to print the footer, select *Footer A* in the Type column and then *Every Page* in the Occurrence column.
4. To begin entering the footer text, press Shift-F6 for centering and type a hyphen (-); then hold Ctrl down and press B. Ctrl-B tells WordPerfect where to print the page number.
5. Type - **(Second Quarter Report/1986)**, and press Enter.
6. Press F7 and then Enter, to get back to regular text mode.

Now enter the text for the second page. When you finish, press Ctrl-Enter to start a new page.

Editing and Canceling Headers and Footers

The Header/Footer Specification menu also includes options that let you edit or cancel a header or footer. To edit one, specify its Type, then choose *Edit* from the Occurrence options. When the header or footer appears, make your changes just as you would with regular text; then press F7 to save the changes.

To cancel a header or footer (i.e., stop it from printing), select *Discontinue* from the Occurrence options. WordPerfect will retain canceled headers and footers; it just won't print them. Thus, you can reactivate one by selecting Occurrence option 1, 2, or 3.

ENTERING THE THIRD PAGE

As Fig. 5-1C shows, the third page consists of two tables. Before entering them, note the following:

- We must change the line spacing back to single spacing.
- We need different tabs for each table, because the columns are spaced differently.
- The tables and titles are centered.

To begin, use the same procedure as before to switch WordPerfect back to single spacing. Now press Shift-F6 to get centering and F6 to get bold type; then enter the title for Table 1 and press F6 to turn off the bold print. Finally, press Enter twice to move the cursor to where the table begins.

Centering a Table

At this point we must create tabs for the table. To determine where they go, we must enter the table headings and the longest line of data, adjust the spacing, center the headings, and move the data under them. The starting points of the data will tell us where to set tabs.

To begin, enter the headings and the first line of data, with three spaces between columns. Remember to press F8 before and after each heading, to underline it. The two lines should look like this:

Region	Units Sold	Revenues ($)	% Change from 1985
Northeast	5,770	2,481,100	+6.7

To adjust the spacing, move the cursor to the U in Units on the first line, and press the space bar three times to put the U directly above the "5" in "5,770". This puts three spaces between the *Units Sold* heading and *Northeast* on the data line.

The insertion spaces the headings correctly. *Revenues ($)* and *% Change from 1985* do not need additional spacing, because they are longer than the entries below them.

Now move the cursor to the *R* in *Region* and press Shift-F6 to center the headings; then press the down-arrow key twice to reach the data line. The screen should show:

Region	Units Sold	Revenues ($)	% Change from 1985
Northeast	5,770	2,481,100	+6.7

We must now put the data items below their headings. To do this, press the space bar until *Northeast* is below *Region*. Now adjust the other three data items in the same way until the screen shows this arrangement:

Region	Units Sold	Revenues ($)	% Change from 1985
Northeast	5,770	2,481,100	+6.7

The tabs belong in the leftmost character position in each data column; these are columns 13, 28, 40, and 61. To set them, move the cursor to the next data line and do the following:

1. Press Shift-F8 to obtain the Line Format menu; then type 1 for Tabs.
2. When the tabs display appears, press Ctrl-End to clear the automatic tabs.
3. To set the new tabs, type **13, 28, 40,** and **61,** and press Enter after each one.
4. Press F7 to return to the document.

After setting the tabs, you can use them on every line except the last two (*Southwest* and *Totals*). You shouldn't use them on the *Southwest* line because you must underline the spaces in front of the data columns. WordPerfect won't let you do that with tabbed material. Similarly, on the Totals line you can't use Tab because some data starts ahead of the tab positions.

You can enter Table 2 in much the same way as Table 1, except you must use different tabs for Table 2. The steps are:

1. Move the cursor to the line where the title goes.
2. Get centering and emboldening; then enter the title.
3. Move the cursor to the line where the headings belong.
4. Enter the headings (underlined) and the top line of data.
5. Insert spaces ahead of the *Sales Rep.* heading until there are two spaces between it and the first column of data.
6. Align the last three data columns under their headings.
7. Record the tab setting for each column; if you followed directions, they should be at columns 13, 25, 41, and 59.
8. Use the Line Format command to obtain the tabs display; then erase the existing tabs (by pressing Ctrl-End) and set new tabs for the data columns.
9. Enter the rest of the table; then press Ctrl-Enter to begin the fourth page.

ENTERING THE FOURTH PAGE

Like the second page of the report, the fourth page (shown in Fig. 5-1D) is double-spaced. Therefore, use the Line Format command key to change the spacing to **2**. Now enter the text. When you finish, press Ctrl-Enter to begin the final page.

ENTERING THE FIFTH PAGE

Page 5 is much like page 3. Once again, you must change the spacing back to *1*. You must also create a centered table with new tabs.

SAVING AND PRINTING A REPORT

After entering the final page, press F10 to save the report on the disk; name it *q286.rpt*. When the *Saving* message disappears, you can print the report. Before doing so, however, you must turn the justification off. To do this, move to the beginning of the document, press Ctrl-F8 to obtain the Print Format menu, type **3** for *Turn off*, and press Enter to leave the menu.

Printing Multiple Copies

You can print at this point, but using the Print command will produce only one copy. To print multiple copies, you must change WordPerfect's print options. For example, we can get nine copies as follows. First, press Shift-F7 to obtain the Print menu. When it appears, type **3** for *Change Options*; this produces

Change Print Options Temporarily	
1 - Printer Number	1
2 - Number of Copies	1
3 - Binding Width (1/10 in.)	0

Selection: 0 appears at the bottom of the screen. Now, type **2** to choose *Number of Copies* (the cursor moves there) and **9** for nine copies; then press Enter twice to get back to the Print menu. Finally, type **1** to select *Full Text*.

Printing Selected Pages

WordPerfect also lets you print selected pages of any document stored on disk. (That can even be the document on the screen, provided you have previously saved it on disk.) To begin, press Shift-F7 to obtain the Print menu and type 4 for *Printer Control*. When WordPerfect displays its Printer Control menu (Fig. 5-3), type p for *Print a Document*. Finally, respond to a series of three prompts that ask for the document name, the starting page (press Enter to start with *1*), and the ending page (press Enter to print to the end of the document).

Printing Blocks of Text

WordPerfect can also print a portion of a page, such as a table or paragraph. To make it do this, move the cursor to where you want the printing to start and press Alt-F4 to put WordPerfect into Block mode. Then move the cursor to the last character you want printed and press Shift-F7 to do a Print command. When the screen shows *Print Block? (Y/N) N*, type y for yes.

Controlling Page Numbering

For the sample report, we let WordPerfect number the pages from the beginning, with the title page being *1*, the second page being *2*, and so on. Some documents, however, have a title page, table of contents, and an introduction or preface. These should be numbered separately, so you want to start numbering on the first page of regular text. To do this, enter a header or footer that includes the symbol ^B on the first page to be numbered.

```
Printer Control                         C - Cancel Print Job(s)
                                        D - Display All Print Jobs
    1 - Select Print Option             G - "Go" (Resume Printing)
    2 - Display Printers and Fonts      P - Print a Document
    3 - Select Printers                 R - Rush Print Jobs
                                        S - Stop Printing
    Selection:  |0|


Current Job
    Job Number:  n/a                    Page Number:    n/a
    Job Status:  n/a                    Current Copy:   n/a

    Message:    The print queue is empty

Job List
Job    Document    Destination      Forms and Print Operations

Additional jobs not shown:  0
```

Fig. 5-3. The Printer Control menu.

WordPerfect assumes you want to number the first header or footer page according to its position in the document. To start with some other number, move the cursor to the first page that has a header or footer, and then do the following:

1. Press Alt-F8 to obtain the Page Format menu.
2. When the menu appears, type 2 for *New Page Number*. WordPerfect displays *New Page #:*.
3. Type the new starting number and press Enter. WordPerfect displays

Numbering Style   1 Arabic;   2 Roman: 0

where Arabic numbers are the regular 1, 2, and 3 kind, while Roman numbers are of the form i, ii, and iii.
4. Choose your numbering style; then press Enter twice to get back to your document.

Working During a Print Operation

As soon as WordPerfect starts printing, it removes the *Please Wait* message and returns you to editing. This means you can actually do other work *during* the print operation! For example, you could select an additional document or a different part of the same one for printing. This makes WordPerfect add the second document to its list of printing jobs and print it immediately after the first one. You could also create a new document or edit an existing one—even one on the print job list!

Stopping a Print Operation

Sometimes you may want to stop a print operation to fix a problem (say, the printer has run out of paper) or cancel the printing entirely. Further, if you spot a mistake in a report or remember something you meant to add, you may want to cancel printing for a particular document (either the current one or another in the print job list).

In either case, begin by pressing Shift-F4 to obtain the Print menu, and type 4 for Printer Control. When WordPerfect displays its Printer Control menu, do one of two things:

- To stop printing temporarily, type **s** for *Stop Printing*. When the printer stops, the Printer Control menu displays the following on the *Message:* line

> Fix printer—Reset top of form—Press "G" to continue

This tells you to fix the problem, advance the paper to the top of the next page, then press **g** for Go. When you press **g**, WordPerfect reprints the page at which it stopped and then completes the job. As soon as it starts printing again, you may press Enter to get back to your document.

- To cancel a print operation, type **c** for *Cancel Print Job(s)*. When requested, enter the number of the job you want to cancel (or * to cancel all jobs); then type **y** to confirm and Enter to leave the Printer Control menu.

SPECIAL PRINT FORMATS

Besides underlining and bold print, WordPerfect can also produce subscripts, superscripts, double underlines, and strikeouts. Subscripts, superscripts, and strikeouts do not appear on the screen; double underlines appear as single underlines.

Subscripts

If your report includes chemical formulas such as H_2O or mathematical notation such as A_i, you will need subscripts that appear below the line. The procedure differs depending on whether you want to subscript new or existing material.

To apply a subscript to new text, begin by pressing Shift and F1 to obtain the following Super/Subscript menu:

> 1 Superscript; 2 Subscript; 3 Overstrike; 6 Adv Up;
> 7 Adv Dn; 8 Adv Ln: 0

What you do next depends on how much material you want to subscript, as follows:

- To subscript the next character you type, enter **2** to select *Subscript* an *s* appears at the bottom left-hand corner; then type the character.
- To subscript the next string of characters you type, enter **5** to select *Adv Dn* (an upside-down triangle appears at the bottom left-hand corner), and type the characters. When you finish typing the subscripted material, press Shift-F1 to get the Super/Subscript menu and enter **4** for *Adv Up*. For example, to pro-

duce H_2O, enter **4**, press Shift-F1 and **5**, type **2**, press Shift-F1 and **4**, and type **O**.

To subscript existing material, put WordPerfect in Block mode and highlight the material; then press Shift-F1 and **2**.

Superscripts

If your report includes footnotes, references, or mathematical formulas such as $E = mc^2$ or $c^3 = a^6 + b^9$, you will need superscripts that appear above the line. As with subscripts, the procedure differs depending on whether you want to superscript new or existing material.

To apply a superscript to new text, press Shift-F1 to obtain the Super/Subscript menu, then do one of the following:

- To superscript the next character you type, enter **1** to select *Superscript* (an *S* appears at the bottom left-hand corner), then type the character. For example, to produce $E = mc^2$, enter **E = mc** , press Shift-F1 and **1**, then type **2**.
- To superscript the next string of characters you type, enter **4** to select *Adv Up* (a triangle appears at the bottom left-hand corner) and type the characters. When you finish typing the superscripted material, press Shift-F1 to get the Super/Subscript menu and enter **5** for *Adv Dn*. Note that this procedure is the reverse of what you do for a subscript.

To superscript existing material, put WordPerfect in Block mode, highlight the material, then press Shift-F1 and **1**.

Double Underlines

In addition to underlining material, WordPerfect can also put a double underline beneath it. To produce this, you must switch WordPerfect's underlining style from single to double. The procedure is: press Ctrl and F8 to obtain the Print Format menu. When it appears, select either *Non-continuous Double* (6) or *Continuous Double* (8); then press Enter. (The non-continuous style does not underline tabs; continuous does.) After that, whenever you underline something, WordPerfect will show a single underline on the screen, but print with a double underline.

WordPerfect keeps using the active underline style until you tell it to use another. Thus, to get back to single underlining, repeat the selection process and choose one of the single styles.

Strikeouts

When lawyers or legislators change a legal document, they often indicate what has been deleted by striking through it with hyphens. WordPerfect provides a strikeout feature that lets you do this.

To apply the strikeout to text, select it in Block mode; then press Alt and F5 to give WordPerfect a *Mark Text* command. When the following menu appears:

Mark for 1 Table of Contents; 2 List; 3 Redline;
4 Strikeout; 5 Index: 0

type **4** for Strikeout. WordPerfect leaves Block mode and returns you to editing.

For example, suppose your will includes the sentence

The estate is to be equally distributed among John, Mary, Elizabeth, and Jason Cane.

Later, in an act of heartless vengeance, you decide to disinherit Elizabeth. To do this, move the cursor to the *E* and press Alt-F4 for Block mode. Then select *Elizabeth*, press Alt-F5 for Mark Text, and type **1** for Strikeout. When you print the will, the sentence will appear as

The estate is to be equally distributed among John, Mary, ~~Elizabeth~~, and Jason Cane.

WordPerfect will strikeout characters with a hyphen (-) unless you tell it to use something else. To change the strikeout character, refer to the Printer Program section of the Installation manual.

Mixing Print Formats

You can apply more than one special print format to a given piece of text. For example, you can embolden an underlined title or embolden a subscript or superscript. To do this, simply apply the first format and then the second. For example, to embolden and underline a title, press F6 and F8, and then enter the title and press F6 and F8 again.

Removing Special Print Formats

In Chapter 3, we discussed removing underlining and centering by deleting their invisible codes in the Reveal Codes mode. You can also use Reveal Codes to remove any of the special print formats we just mentioned. Simply move the cursor to where the format starts and press Alt-F3 to obtain the Reveal Codes display; then delete the code.

WordPerfect precedes each subscripted or superscripted character with [SubScrpt] or [SuprScrpt]; make sure you delete all of them. It also precedes double-underlined text with [U], and at the point where you switched to the double style, either [Undrl Style:6] (for Non-continuous Double) or [Undrl Style:8] (for Continuous Double). Finally, WordPerfect precedes strikeout text with [StrkOut].

If you have applied more than one format, the cursor ([^]) may not be next to the code you want to delete. That's no problem. Use the arrow keys to move it, then delete the code by pressing Del if the cursor precedes the code or Backspace if the cursor follows it. Finally, press Enter to leave the Reveal Codes display.

FOOTNOTES AND ENDNOTES

WordPerfect lets you add footnotes to any page. Once you have created a footnote, WordPerfect automatically numbers it and "attaches" it to the text that refers to it. That is, if changes move the reference to a different page, WordPerfect moves the footnote along with it. Similarly, if you delete a footnote reference, WordPerfect deletes its footnote as well. *Endnotes* are the same as footnotes, except WordPerfect puts them at the end of the document.

Footnotes do not appear on the screen during regular editing (nor do endnotes), but WordPerfect prints them at the bottom of the page where their references appear. It also prints a line above the footnotes, to set them off from the regular text.

Creating Notes

To create either kind of note (footnote or endnote), move the cursor to where you want the note number inserted; then press Ctrl and F7 to give a Footnote command. When this menu appears:

```
1 Create; 2 Edit; 3 New #; 4 Options; 5 Create Endnote;
6 Edit Endnote: 0
```

type 1 to create a footnote or **5** to create an endnote. WordPerfect shows a clear screen that looks like the one you use to create a header or footer. It has a number at the top—the reference number WordPerfect has assigned to this note—and *Press EXIT when done* at the bottom. Enter the text for your note; then press the F7 (Exit) key to return to the regular text. Now WordPerfect has put the reference number at the place where you pressed Ctrl-F7.

For example, suppose you are writing a term paper on "Alaskan Explorers" that includes the sentence

Their journey took them through the Shelikov Strait.

and you want "Shelikov Strait" to refer to the footnote

A strait 30 miles wide between the Alaskan Peninsula and the Kodiak and Afognak Islands.

To put this footnote at the bottom of the page, enter the reference sentence, and then press Ctrl-F7 and type **1** for *Create*. When the blank screen appears, enter the footnote text and press F7.

When you print the term paper, the reference sentence will appear in the text in this form:

Their journey took them through the Shelikov Strait.[1]

and the footnote will appear at the bottom of the page in this form:

---

[1]A strait 30 miles wide between the Alaskan Peninsula and the Kodiak and Afognak Islands.

(Of course, the superscript *1* here assumes that this is the first footnote in the term paper. If other footnotes precede it, the reference number will be higher.)

Editing Notes

You can edit a note from anywhere in your document. To begin, press Ctrl-F7 to obtain the Footnote menu; then type **2** for a footnote or **6** for an endnote. WordPerfect displays *Ftn #?* or *Endn #?*, followed by a number. If this is number of the note you want to edit, press Enter; otherwise, type the correct number and then press Enter. When WordPerfect displays the note, make your changes, and press F7 to get back to editing.

Deleting Notes

To delete a note, put the cursor on its reference number in the text and press

Del. When WordPerfect asks *Delete [Note]? (Y/N) N*, type **y**. Deleting the number also deletes the note it refers to. Of course, if you accidentally delete a note, you can undelete it by pressing F1 (Cancel) then typing **1** for *Restore*.

ALIGNING DECIMAL NUMBERS

WordPerfect lets you use tabs to mark the position of the decimal point in a column of numbers. When you press Ctrl and F6 (rather than Tab) to reach a tab position, WordPerfect moves the cursor and shows *Align Char = .* at the bottom of the screen. Then WordPerfect automatically aligns the number you enter there. That is, it shifts everything left until you type a decimal point, then puts anything else you enter to the right.

For example, suppose your organization is rasing money for a charity and you want to list how much each member has collected:

~ Member	Collections ~
Brown, John	$1,504.36
Carlson, Ray	965.77
Decker, Patricia	1,668.43
Garnett, Vance	769.03
Evans, Sue	779.56
Gerard, Roy	1,056.90
Morton, Mary	800.00
Stevens, George	863.96

You must set a tab directly below the "t" in *Collections*. Then you simply press Ctrl-F6 (Tab Align) after entering each name, and type the amount. WordPerfect will align it automatically around the tab position.

For example, as you enter **$1,504** on the first line, WordPerfect will put each character at the tab position and shift all preceding characters left. Then, when you type the decimal point, WordPerfect will stop shifting and put the next two digits (**36**) to the right of the decimal point.

INDENTING LISTS

When people type a list of items, they often indent them and set them off with numbers, dashes, or *bullets*. For example, suppose you want to indent three numbered sentences in a letter, as in

In response to your recent request, we need the following
information to complete a credit application:

    1) Name and address of your bank, along with your account
       number.
    2) Three credit references.

3) A signed corporate resolution indicating responsibility
   for payment.

To indent material, simply set a tab where you want the indented left-hand margin. Then, whenever you want to indent something, press F4 (rather than Tab) to start indenting. WordPerfect will indent everything you type until you press Enter. In other words, it will indent a paragraph's worth of text.

You can also indent a paragraph you entered earlier. To do this, put the cursor on the first character and press F4. Of course, if you have a tab at the beginning of a paragraph, you simply press F4 at the left-hand margin rather than the first character. Either way, WordPerfect will indent only the current paragraph.

MULTICOLUMN MATERIAL

Newspaper and magazine articles, newsletters, dramatic scripts, and some legal documents are printed with several columns on a page. WordPerfect lets you produce two different kinds of column styles. *Newspaper-style columns* are designed for text that continues from one column to the next, in winding fashion. You may want to use this style for a newsletter. *Parallel columns* are designed to keep different information together on a page. You could use this style to produce a script, resume, or inventory list.

WordPerfect can handle up to five columns on a page, and can divide them into equal-spaced columns (you tell it how many spaces to put between columns) or place them according to column margins you specify. WordPerfect shows all of the columns on the screen.

To put WordPerfect into either text column mode, press Alt and F7 for Math/Columns. When the menu appears, type **4** for Column Def. WordPerfect shows a form you fill out to specify the width and type of columns you want. When you complete it, and the menu reappears, type **3** for *Column On/Off.*

Entering Newspaper-Style Columns

When entering newspaper-style columns, you simply keep typing. WordPerfect will advance to the next column when the current one is full, and will start a new page when the last column is full. When you finish entering column material, press Alt-F7 to obtain the menu and type **3** to turn columns off.

Entering Parallel Columns

When entering Parallel Columns, you type what you want into the first column and then press Ctrl-Enter to move to the next column. Another Ctrl-Enter takes you to the next column, if there is one. If you press it from the rightmost column, WordPerfect moves the cursor to the first column—*not* to the next page.

To start a new page with parallel columns, press Alt-F7 to obtain the menu and type **3** to turn columns off. Then press Ctrl-Enter to start the next page. Word-

Perfect is in regular text mode on the new page. To enter more columns, get the menu again and select *Columns On/Off.*

HANDLING LONG REPORTS

Hard disks can hold millions of characters (i.e., thousands of pages), so hard disk users rarely run out of space for their documents. Floppy disk users, however, can run out of storage space by filling the data disk. Hence, if you are using floppy disks, you should have an idea about the amount of storage available.

With WordPerfect, a floppy disk can hold about 70 single-spaced pages or 140 double-spaced pages. Therefore, a long report may not fit entirely on one disk.

If you try to save a document on a full disk, WordPerfect displays

Disk full - Strike any key to continue

at the bottom of the screen. When that happens, you can either try saving on another formatted data disk or make room on the current disk by removing documents you no longer need. For details on how to remove documents from a disk, see "Deleting Documents" in Chapter 2.

Organizing Long Reports

The most efficient way to organize long reports is to create a separate document for each section or chapter. This not only gives you logical stopping points if you need to switch to a new disk, but also lets you make changes to one section without affecting others.

COPYING DOCUMENTS

WordPerfect keeps only one copy of a document on your data disk. Therefore, if you lose that disk, spill something on it, or destroy it in some other way, all of your work disappears. For safety's sake, you should make a *backup* copy of important documents and keep the backup disk in a safe place, out of harm's way.

You may also want to copy to create a different version of a document. For example, you might have a standard contract form and variations for common situations. You might also have wholesale, retail, and promotional price lists.

WordPerfect lets you copy a document onto any disk, as long as it's formatted. To begin, press F5 to List Files. When the list appears, move the light bar to the file you want to copy and press **8** for Copy. WordPerfect asks

Copy this File to:

To copy to the same disk, enter the name you want the copy to have; then press Enter twice to get back to editing. To copy to a different disk, put it in drive A (replacing the WordPerfect disk), then enter **a:** and the name of the copy (e.g., **a:jackson.let**). Insert the WordPerfect disk and press Enter twice to get back to editing. If you are copying to a different disk, the name can be the same as before. If you are copying to the same disk, you must give the copy a different name.

PRODUCING BACKUP FILES

WordPerfect can also make backups automatically if you tell it to. To make it do this, start the computer as usual, but when the B> prompt appears, enter **a:wp/s** (instead of **a:wp**). When the Set-Up Menu appears, enter **4** for *Set Backup Options*. WordPerfect provides options it calls *Timed Backup* and *Original Backup*.

Timed Backup

The Timed Backup option guards against an unexpected power failure, by saving the active document at regular intervals. Each time, it stores the document in a file named {WP}BACK.1. Then, if the power ever goes off when Word-Perfect is running, restart it (see "Starting WordPerfect After a Power Failure" in Chapter 2), retrieve {WP}BACK.1, and save it under the original name.

Original Backup

The Original Backup option makes WordPerfect create a backup when you save a document. In doing this, WordPerfect gives the backup the same name, but with the extension *.BK!*. For example, if you save a document named ros-ter.doc, WordPerfect saves the new version as ROSTER.DOC and the original as ROSTER.BK!.

If you somehow foul up a document beyond repair, you may want to go back to the original. To do this, retrieve the backup (.BK!) file, and then save it under the original name.

QUESTIONS AND ANSWERS

Question: How can I make WordPerfect print something emboldened and underlined?

Answer: Press F6 and F8, type the text, and then press F6 and F8 again.

Question: My report is a combination of four different documents. The first page of each one includes the footer - *Page* ^B - to number the pages. When I print them, WordPerfect always numbers the first page *1*. How can I make it give the entire report consecutive page numbers?

Answer: Before you print the second, third, and fourth documents, press Alt-F8 to obtain the Page Format menu and type **2** for *New Page Number*. When asked for the *New Page #*, enter the starting page number for the document. For example, if each document is 20 pages long, enter **21** for the second one, **41** for the third, and **61** for the fourth.

Question: I made some changes to pages 20 and 21 of my report. How can I print just those two pages?

Answer: Save the report on disk and press Shift-F7 to start the printing procedure. When WordPerfect displays its Print menu, type **4** for *Printer Control* and then **p** for *Print a Document*. Enter the report's name, **20** for the *Starting page*, and **21** for the *Ending page*. Since page 20 is deep in the heart of the document, it may take a while for WordPerfect to reach it.

Question: I want to print copies of five different letters from my disk. Do I have to wait until each letter has been printed before I can tell WordPerfect which one to print next?

Answer: No, you can simply give WordPerfect a series of print commands, one for each letter. That is, start the first print operation. Then do another print operation and tell WordPerfect which document you want to print next. Continue doing this for the other three letters. WordPerfect remembers each print command and performs them in the order you specified.

Question: How can I indent a paragraph on both sides?

Answer: Before you type the paragraph, obtain the Line Format menu and set tabs where you want the left and right indentation (remember to delete any existing tabs that precede the left tab or follow the right tab). Then press Shift and F4 to give a *Left/Right Indent* command and type the paragraph. WordPerfect will indent both sides of it. When you finish, change the tabs back to where you want them for the rest of the text.

Question: I double underlined a word for emphasis, using a Print Format command to switch to *Non-continuous Double* style. The problem is, I forgot to switch back to single underlining, and now the rest of my report is filled with double underlines. What can I do?

Answer: Move the cursor to where you want the double underlining to stop, then do another Print Format command and select one of the single styles (5 or 7). WordPerfect will return to single underlining at that point, as you'll see when you next print the report.

HINTS AND WARNINGS

1. To enter a centered table, type its headings and a line of data before determining the tab positions.

2. When using a special print format (bold print, subscript, superscript, or double underscore), be sure to turn the format off at the end of the affected material.

3. Underlining and bold print will appear on the screen, but subscripts, superscripts, and strikeouts will not. Double-underlined material appears with a single underline.

4. Do not enter material with a tab if you must enter anything to the left of the tab position. WordPerfect will not let you do it.

5. If you print selected pages of a document using the Print command's *Printer Control* option, you can print to the end of the document by pressing Enter in response to the *Ending page* prompt.

6. If you try to save a document on a full disk, WordPerfect displays a *Disk full* message. When that happens, you must either insert a different disk and try saving again or remove some documents from the current disk. To guard against filling a disk, you can use the List Files command to find out how much disk space is still available; WordPerfect reports it at the top of the List Files screen.

7. To move a document from one disk to another, copy it to the second disk and then delete it from the first disk.

8. If you lose a disk or some other misfortune befalls it, you're out of luck unless you have a backup. Create backup copies of all your important documents by periodically copying them to another disk.

9. When entering information as Parallel Columns, be careful not to type past line 54, the bottom of the page. If you do, WordPerfect moves the overflow material to the next column, just as it does with newspaper-style columns.

KEY POINT SUMMARY

Table 5-1 summarizes the keys we introduced in this chapter.

1. To embolden text, press F6 before and after it.

2. To double space text, change the Line Format menu's *Spacing* value to *2*.

3. To create a header or footer for a document, put the cursor at the top of the first page where you want one and press Alt-F8 and Enter. Choose *Headers or Footers*; then specify the Type and Occurrence. Finally, enter the text and press F7 (Exit) at the end of the final line.

4. To include the page number in a header or footer, enter Ctrl-B where you want it to appear.

5. To change the tabs or margins within a page, do a Line Format command and select *Tabs* or *Margins*. WordPerfect will reformat the text between this format change and the next one.

6. Options on the Print menu allow you to produce multiple copies (Change Options) and print selected pages (Printer Control).

7. To specify the starting page number for a header or footer that includes the page number symbol ^B, select *New Page Number* from the Page Format menu.

Table 5-1. Keys Introduced in Chapter 5.

Key(s)	Function
Shift-F1	Super/Subscript
F4	Indent
Shift-F4	Left/Right Indent
Alt-F5	Mark Text
F6	Bold print
Ctrl-F6	Tab Align (align number around decimal point)
Alt-F7	Math/Columns
Ctrl-F7	Footnote

8. Once printing has begun, you can create a new document or edit an existing one.

9. To stop a print operation, obtain the Print menu and select *Printer Control*. When the Printer Control menu appears, type **s** to stop printing temporarily or **c** to cancel a job.

10. To produce a superscript or subscript, press Shift-F1 to obtain the Super/Subscript menu. Options in the menu allow you to apply a superscript or subscript to the next character you type (option 1 or 2) or to the next string of characters you type (4 to begin and 5 to end or 5 to begin and 4 to end).

11. To apply a superscript or subscript to existing material, select it in Block mode; then press Shift-F1 and either **1** or **2**.

12. To double underscore material, select a Double underlining style from the Print Format menu.

13. To strikeout material (print hyphens through it), select it in Block mode and press Alt-F5 for *Mark Text*; then press **4** for *Strikeout.*

14. You can remove any of the special print formats just as you remove underlining—by deleting the format's code. This involves using the Reveal Codes command.

15. WordPerfect can produce both footnotes and endnotes. Footnotes are printed on the same page as their reference number, while endnotes are printed at the end of the document.

16. To create a footnote or endnote, enter the reference text and press Ctrl-F7 to give a *Footnote* command; then press **1** (Create) for a footnote or **5** (Create Endnote) for an endnote. When the blank screen appears, enter the text for the note, then press F7 to get back to editing.

17. You can also edit a note by selecting *Edit* (2) or *Edit Endnote* (6) from the Footnote menu. To obtain the text of the note, enter its number when requested. To delete a note, simply delete its reference number.

18. The *Tab Align* command (Ctrl-F6) allows you to align columns of numbers around a decimal point.

19. You can change a paragraph's left-hand margin by indenting it. To do this, set a tab and press F4 (Indent) to reach it. WordPerfect will indent the next paragraph you enter.

20. You can also indent a paragraph on both the left and right side. To do this, set the left-hand and right-hand tabs; then press Shift-F4 (Left/Right Indent) to reach the left indentation and enter the paragraph.

21. WordPerfect can produce up to five columns of text on a page in either of two text-column styles. Newspaper-style columns continue text from one column to the next, in winding fashion. Parallel columns let you enter different material into side-by-side columns.

    To put WordPerfect into a column mode, press Alt-F7 to obtain the *Math/Columns* menu. The *Column Def* option lets you specify the column type and spacing; the *Column On/Off* option lets you turn the column mode on or off.

22. The List Files menu's *Copy* option lets you copy documents. Copying provides a backup capability and a starting point for new documents.

23. WordPerfect can produce backup copies of documents automatically. The Set-Up Menu lets you choose whether WordPerfect is to produce a backup at regular intervals (Timed Backup) or when you save a document (Original Backup).

Chapter 6

Revising

In the preceding chapters you learned how to change and correct characters, words, lines, sentences, and paragraphs. Formal correspondence, reports, and large projects, however, often require more extensive revisions.

For example, you may want to move material to improve continuity, combine related ideas or separate distinct ones, change emphasis, or balance the length of sections. Or you may need the same legal or technical terminology, table or figure heading, address, equation, or set of instructions in several places. You may also want to find occurrences of certain words, phrases, or sequences in a document, and perhaps change them to correct spelling, improve grammar, standardize terminology, or change dates, names, places, numbers, or titles.

MOVE AND COPY OPERATIONS

WordPerfect can move or copy sentences, paragraphs, pages, blocks of text, or columns within tables. You move text in WordPerfect much as you would in a rough draft of a typed document; that is, you cut it from one place and paste it in another—but with WordPerfect, you cut and paste electronically. Copying text is the same as moving it, except you leave the original in place.

Sentences, Paragraphs, and Pages

To move or copy a sentence, paragraph, or page, put the cursor anywhere within it, and then do the following:

1. Press Ctrl-F4 to give WordPerfect a Move command. This produces the following menu

> Move 1 Sentence; 2 Paragraph; 3 Page; **Retrieve** 4 Column;
> 5 Text; 6 Rectangle: 0

2. Type **1**, **2**, or **3**. WordPerfect highlights the sentence, paragraph, or page, and displays

> 1 Cut; 2 Copy: 0

3. To move the unit, type **1** for Cut; to leave it in place, type **2** for Copy. If you selected Cut, the unit disappears and WordPerfect automatically closes the gap where it was.
4. If the destination is on another page, use Ctrl-Home (Go to), PgUp, or PgDn to move there.
5. Move the cursor to where you want the unit to go and press Ctrl-F4 again.
6. When the Move/Retrieve menu appears, type **5** for Text. WordPerfect pastes the unit at the cursor position.

How WordPerfect Defines Sentences and Paragraphs

One problem with WordPerfect is that it does not always define sentences and paragraphs the way people think of them. This can produce surprising results when you select text for moving or copying.

WordPerfect defines a *sentence* as all characters from the beginning up to and including the next period, exclamation point, question mark, or quotation mark. This also takes in any spaces following the concluding punctuation mark. For example, the sentence "Mr. F. Scott Fitzgerald isn't home." is three sentences to WordPerfect, because it cannot tell the periods after Mr. and F. from the period at the end of the sentence.

Likewise, a *paragraph* is everything from just after the last Enter, up to and including the next Enter. This will not be an entire paragraph if there are extra Enters because of equations, titles, lists, or quoted material. Thus WordPerfect may well treat one paragraph as several, and it will also think of each equation, title, list entry, quotation, or other material set off by Enters as a paragraph by itself.

The moral here is simple. Always watch the screen when you select a sentence or paragraph. Sometimes the results will not be what you might expect. Don't proceed under the assumption that WordPerfect thinks the way you do. If you don't like what WordPerfect has selected, you should move or copy the text by first defining it as a block.

Blocks

To move or copy a block of text, put the cursor at the beginning of it and proceed as follows:

1. Press Alt-F4 to put WordPerfect in Block mode.
2. Select (highlight) the block, then press Ctrl-F4 to do a *Move* command. Word-Perfect displays the following menu:

1 Cut Block; 2 Copy Block; 3 Append; 4 Cut/Copy Column;
5 Cut/Copy Rectangle: 0

3. To move the block, type **1** for Cut Block; to leave it in place, type **2** for Copy Block. If you selected Cut Block, the block disappears and WordPerfect automatically closes the gap where it was.
4. If the destination is on another page, use Ctrl-Home (Go to), PgUp, or PgDn to move there.
5. Move the cursor to where you want the block and press Ctrl-F4 again. Word-Perfect pastes it there.
6. When the following menu appears:

Move 1 Sentence; 2 Paragraph; 3 Page; Retrieve 4 Column;
5 Text; 6 Rectangle: 0

type **5** for Text. WordPerfect pastes the block at the cursor position.

For example, suppose you are typing the following text:

> Our firm specializes in tax-advantaged investments such as oil and gas exploration and development, equipment leasing, and real estate.
>
> Our background in oil and gas exploration and development includes over 50 projects during the last ten years.

When you start the new paragraph, you notice the repetition of "oil and gas exploration and development". Rather than typing it again, move the cursor up to the "o" in "oil" and get into Block mode, then highlight to the "t" in "development" and do a Move command with the Copy option. Now put the cursor back where it was (two spaces past "in") and do another Move, but this time choose **5** to Retrieve Text. The original phrase is still in place, and a copy appears in the text.

Note that the phrase remains in memory in case you need it again. (In that case, do another Move and select Retrieve Text.)

Columns

To move or copy a column of text or numbers, start as you would for a block; that is, obtain Block mode and highlight everything between the beginning and end of the column. (Of course, doing that makes WordPerfect highlight other columns in the table as well.) Then press Ctrl and F4 to do a Move command. When the Move/Retrieve menu appears, type 4 for Cut/Copy Column. To paste the column, do another Move and select Column (option 4) from the menu.

Adjusting the Format

When you move or copy text using the procedures we just gave, it takes on the line format settings (tabs, margins, and spacing) that are active at the new location. This means, for example, that if you move single-spaced material to a double-spaced page, WordPerfect makes it double-spaced.

To restore the original format, perform the move or copy and then correct the format at the new location by doing Line Format commands just before and just after the moved material. (Note that the number of Line Format commands depends on whether the tabs, margins, and spacing differ between the moved text and the destination text.) The Line Formats that precede the moved text should restore the original format; the ones that follow the text should restore the destination format.

COLUMN OPERATIONS

In the previous section, we described moving and copying columns of text or numbers. WordPerfect can also insert or delete columns. These operations can save a lot of time when you want to manipulate a table.

Inserting Columns

To insert a column into a table, proceed as follows:

1. Insert the heading for the new column.
2. Use Reveal Codes to find the [Tab Set:] code where you set the tabs for the table. Move the cursor just beyond that code and press Enter to get back to editing.
3. Do a Line Format command (Shift-F8) and select the Tabs option.
4. Change the tabs to reflect an additional column. That is, set a tab for the new column and move the remaining tabs right to provide space for the insertion. (To move a tab right, delete it, then set it at its new location.) Finally, return to editing.
5. Put the cursor on the first data line; then move it to where the new column should start.
6. Enter the first data item in the new column, then press Tab to shift the remaining columns to the right.
7. Enter the rest of the data items in the new column by repeating steps 5 and 6.

Column Insert Example

As an example, suppose you have prepared a list of your company's major customers, as shown in Fig. 6-1. As usual, you used tabs at the beginning of each column to enter the data. Here, they are at columns 25 and 42.

After finishing the list, you decide to insert a column for the buyer's telephone number between Buyer and Sales Rep.. Since each number is 12 characters long, and you want three spaces between it the next column, the new column must be 15 characters wide. To insert it, proceed as follows:

1. Put the cursor on the heading line and press Alt-F3 for Reveal Codes.

```
Account         Buyer             Sales Rep.

Wilburg Sons    Paul Wilkinson    R. Roberts
Jenco           Carrie Black      C. Chamber
Symtech         Wayne Beck        P. Grogan
Chicago Gear    Morris Daley      J. Wilkes
Hart Foods      Sandy Karras      P. Wallach
Pacifico        Bill Anderson     D. Kim
Storr Bros.     Lee Walters       B. Lloyd
```

Fig. 6-1. The customer list before column insertion.

2. Move the cursor just beyond the [Tab Set: 25,42] code; then press Enter to leave Reveal Codes.
3. Use the Tabs option of the Line Format command to set a new tab at column 57 (this is where the Sales Rep. column will move after the insertion).

Now you can enter the heading and data for the telephone number column. The final list will look similar to Fig. 6-2.

Deleting Columns

To delete a column, move the cursor to the beginning of it and proceed as follows:

1. Press Alt-F4 to put WordPerfect in the Block mode.
2. Move the cursor to the last character of the column. WordPerfect highlights everything between the first and last characters of the column, even other columns.
3. Press Ctrl-F4 to do a Move. WordPerfect displays the following:

1 Cut Block; 2 Copy Block; 3 Append; 4 Cut/Copy Column;
5 Cut/Copy Rectangle: 0

4. Type 4 for *Cut/Copy Column*. WordPerfect highlights the column and shows

1 Cut; 2 Copy: 0

5. Type 1 for *Cut*. WordPerfect closes the gap by moving the remaining columns to the left.

Moving and Copying Columns

To move a column, follow the same procedure we just gave for deleting one; then move the cursor to where you want the column and press Ctrl-F4 for Move. When the Move/Retrieve menu appears, type 4 for *Column*.

Copying a column is the same as moving one, except you select *Copy* instead of *Cut*.

```
Account          Buyer            Phone #          Sales Rep.

Wilburg Sons     Paul Wilkinson   212-555-3589     R. Roberts
Jenco            Carrie Black     904-388-6743     C. Chamber
Symtech          Wayne Beck       404-783-8832     P. Grogan
Chicago Gear     Morris Daley     312-395-1904     J. Wilkes
Hart Foods       Sandy Karras     406-184-5683     P. Wallach
Pacifico         Bill Anderson    503-438-9532     D. Kim
Storr Bros.      Lee Walters      213-679-4260     B. Lloyd
```

Fig. 6-2. The customer list with inserted columns.

SEARCH AND REPLACE OPERATIONS

WordPerfect has Search commands that search forward or backward through a document looking for a *string* (any sequence of characters). It also has a Replace command that both searches for a string and replaces it. You can use these features to do the following:

- Locate a customer's name in a mailing list.
- Correct a common misspelling throughout a document.
- Update a document to account for changes in names, titles, dates, or locations.
- Change prices, rates, or terms in an invoice or contract.
- Change a part number or order number in a technical manual.
- Replace an overused or inappropriate phrase throughout a report.
- Check for occurrences of obsolete or revised names, titles, dates, or terms.

Searching

The procedure to search for a string is:

1. Move the cursor to where you want the search to begin and press F2 to search forward or Shift-F2 to search backward. WordPerfect displays -> *Srch :* or <- *Srch:* at the bottom of the screen.
2. Type the search string, then press F2 to start searching. The form of the search string determines what WordPerfect will search for. Specifically:

   - If you type the search string in lowercase form, WordPerfect will search for every occurrence of it.
   - If you type it in capitalized form, WordPerfect will only search for capitalized occurrences.

For example, suppose you want to search for the phrase *oil well*. To find every instance of it (i.e., *oil well, Oil Well,* and *OIL WELL*), type **oil well** the string. To find only capitalized instances, (i.e., *Oil Well* and *OIL WELL*), type **Oil well** as the string.

Either way, *don't* press Enter after you type the search string. Pressing Enter would make WordPerfect search only for occurrences that are followed by an Enter—those at the ends of paragraphs. (If you accidentally press Enter, WordPerfect shows it as the code [HRt], for Hard Return; press Backspace to delete the code.)

3. If WordPerfect finds an instance of the string, it puts the cursor just past the last character. Your options at this point are:

   a. To search for the next occurrence of the string, press F2 *twice*.
   b. To return to your starting location, press Ctrl-Home (Go to) *twice*.

If WordPerfect cannot find the string, it leaves the cursor at its original location and displays * *Not found* * on the bottom line.

Changing the Search String

Once you have done a search, WordPerfect assumes you want to look for the same string the next time. This is convenient if you want to resume a search after making changes or corrections, but if you actually want to search for a different string, you must type it directly over the old one.

Selecting Search Strings

If the string you are looking for is long or distinctive, such as "International Products Division" or "NASA", you probably won't have any trouble with unexpected matches. If it is not distinctive, however, WordPerfect may stop at places you never intended. For example, if you tell WordPerfect to search through a report on cigarette smoking for each mention of "tar", it will stop at "target", "start", "retarding", and "Tarleton".

One solution to this problem is to put a space in front of the string. For example, you could tell WordPerfect to search for " tar". If you put a space after "tar", WordPerfect will not find occurrences followed by a period, a comma, or other punctuation. Even a space in front can cause problems with occurrences such as "(*tar*)".

Replacing

If you have a specific replacement in mind, you should use WordPerfect's Replace command. Replace will even make all the changes automatically, if you are sure there are no exceptions. You can make WordPerfect search and replace as follows:

1. Move the cursor to where you want the search to start and press Alt-F2. Word-Perfect displays *w/Confirm? (Y/N) N* at the bottom of the screen.
2. You have three options:

   - To make WordPerfect replace all occurrences of the search string automatically, type n or press Enter (this is called a *global* search and replace operation).
   - To make WordPerfect stop each time it finds the string and ask if you want to replace it, type y.
   - To cancel the Replace operation, press F1.

   If you type n or y, WordPerfect shows -> *Srch* on the bottom line.

3. Type the string you want to search for (but don't press Enter at the end of it), then press F2. WordPerfect shows *Replace with:* on the bottom line.
4. Enter the replacement string, then press F2.

   Note that you can just press F2 here if you want to replace the string with nothing (i.e., delete it). You might do this, for example, to update someone's title from "Assistant Vice-President" to "Vice-President" throughout a report or interview. Here, you should search for "Assistant" and replace it with nothing.

WordPerfect begins searching when you press F2. If *w/Confirm?* is *Y*, it stops at each instance of the search string and shows the prompt *Confirm? (Y/N) N*. Type y to replace the string, and n to proceed to the next occurrence, or F1 to cancel the replace operation. If WordPerfect cannot find another occurrence of the search string, it leaves the cursor where you last started searching and displays * *Not Found* *.

Replace Example

Figure 6-3 shows a document that illustrates the use of the replace options. We want to update this notice for the 1986 annual meeting to be held at the same place on Friday, June 6, 1986. To do this, we will perform the following operations:

1. Replace automatically each occurrence of "1985-86" with "1986-87".
2. Replace automatically each occurrence of "June 7" with "June 6".
3. Find all occurrences of "1985" and replace them with "1986". We must be careful here to avoid changing historical dates accidentally.

To replace "1985-86" automatically with "1986-87", do the following:

1. Put the cursor at the beginning of the first line of the text and then press Alt-F2.
2. In response to *w/Confirm? (Y/N) N*, press Enter to accept *N*.

```
NOTICE OF STOCKHOLDERS' MEETING

     The 1985 Annual Stockholders' Meeting for International
Consolidated Industries will be held at company headquarters,
19850 Pine Street, Des Moines, Iowa on Friday, June 7, 1985.  The
following matters will be considered:

     1)   Election of the Board of Directors for the 1985-86
          fiscal year.
     2)   Designation of Smith, Brown, and Little as the company's
          independent auditors for the 1985-86 fiscal year.
     3)   Amendments to the Employees' Qualified Stock Ownership
          Plan (ESOP) in accordance with new regulations.
     4)   Other amendments and matters as they may be brought to
          the attention of the Secretary of the Corporation.

     Anyone wishing to have matters considered at that meeting
must notify the Secretary by registered mail on or before May 15,
1985.  In accordance with regulations adopted at the annual
meeting of June 11, 1982, such notifications must be presented on
forms provided by the Secretary and must contain notarized
signatures representing no fewer than 1% of the common stock of
the Corporation of record May 15th, 1985.  In accordance with
guidelines adopted at a special Board of Directors meeting on
February 1, 1985, the board has the final authority on whether to
accept notifications that are presented after May 15th, 1985 or
that contain an insufficient number of signatures.
```

Fig. 6-3. The original search document.

3. For -> *Srch:*, type **1985-86**, and press F2. (Note that WordPerfect encloses the hyphen in brackets, as [-]. Don't worry about this, it's normal.)

4. For *Replace with*, type **1986-87** and press F2 again.

WordPerfect immediately makes the replacements and leaves the cursor at the last occurrence. Press the − (minus) key on the numeric keypad to reach the top of the screen.

To replace *June 7* with *June 6*, start by pressing Alt-F2 and n to select automatic (global) replacement. For -> *Srch:*, enter **June 7**, then press F2. Enter the **June 6** replacement string similarly. Now the meeting notice looks like the one shown in Fig. 6-4.

To replace *1985* with *1986* selectively, proceed as follows:

1. Press − to reach the top of the screen.
2. Press Alt-F2 to start a new Replace operation.

3. In response to *w/Confirm? (Y/N) N*, type **y** for yes.
4. For *-> Srch:*, type **1985**; then press F2.
5. For *Replace with*, type **1986**, then F2 again.

WordPerfect will immediately find a match in the second word. You must press **y** to make the replacement.

The next match is unexpected: WordPerfect finds *1985* at the beginning of the company's address. Here you must press **n** to make WordPerfect continue forward without replacing it. You must do this again later when WordPerfect finds *1985* as part of *a special Board of Directors meeting on February 1, 1985,*. That is a historical date, and you must not change it.

When WordPerfect finishes, the document looks like the one shown in Fig. 6-5.

How Search Strings Affect Replace Operations

Under Searching, we mentioned that the form of the search string tells Word-

---

NOTICE OF STOCKHOLDERS' MEETING

The 1985 Annual Stockholders' Meeting for International Consolidated Industries will be held at company headquarters, 19850 Pine Street, Des Moines, Iowa on Friday, June 6, 1985. The following matters will be considered:

1) Election of the Board of Directors for the 1986-87 fiscal year.
2) Designation of Smith, Brown, and Little as the company's independent auditors for the 1986-87 fiscal year.
3) Amendments to the Employees' Qualified Stock Ownership Plan (ESOP) in accordance with new regulations.
4) Other amendments and matters as they may be brought to the attention of the Secretary of the Corporation.

Anyone wishing to have matters considered at that meeting must notify the Secretary by registered mail on or before May 15, 1985. In accordance with regulations adopted at the annual meeting of June 11, 1982, such notifications must be presented on forms provided by the Secretary and must contain notarized signatures representing no fewer than 1% of the common stock of the Corporation of record May 15th, 1985. In accordance with guidelines adopted at a special Board of Directors meeting on February 1, 1985, the board has the final authority on whether to accept notifications that are presented after May 15th, 1985 or that contain an insufficient number of signatures.

Fig. 6-4. The revised document after automatic insertions.

```
              NOTICE OF STOCKHOLDERS' MEETING

    The 1986 Annual Stockholders' Meeting for International
Consolidated Industries will be held at company headquarters,
19850 Pine Street, Des Moines, Iowa on Friday, June 6, 1986.  The
following matters will be considered:

    1)   Election of the Board of Directors for the 1986-87
         fiscal year.
    2)   Designation of Smith, Brown, and Little as the company's
         independent auditors for the 1986-87 fiscal year.
    3)   Amendments to the Employees' Qualified Stock Ownership
         Plan (ESOP) in accordance with new regulations.
    4)   Other amendments and matters as they may be brought to
         the attention of the Secretary of the Corporation.

    Anyone wishing to have matters considered at that meeting
must notify the Secretary by registered mail on or before May 15,
1986.  In accordance with regulations adopted at the annual
meeting of June 11, 1982, such notifications must be presented on
forms provided by the Secretary and must contain notarized
signatures representing no fewer than 1% of the common stock of
the Corporation of record May 15th, 1986.  In accordance with
guidelines adopted at a special Board of Directors meeting on
February 1, 1985, the board has the final authority on whether to
accept notifications that are presented after May 15th, 1986 or
that contain an insufficient number of signatures.
```

Fig. 6-5. The final form of the document.

Perfect what to search for. (A lowercase string makes it search for every occurrence, while an uppercase string makes it search only for capitalized occurrences.) For Replace operations, the search string can affect what WordPerfect replaces as well as what it finds.

When replacing, WordPerfect uses the following guidelines:

- If the search string consists of lowercase characters, WordPerfect finds every occurrence of it and replaces that occurrence with your replacement string exactly.
- If the search string contains an uppercase character, WordPerfect finds occurrences in which the same character is capitalized and replaces it with the *matching* form of your replacement string.

This can cause problems in some Replace operations. For example, suppose you have prepared a letter using the singular form (e.g., "I would like . . ." and

"Still, I want . . ."), and your spouse or business partner asks you to change every *I* to we. To do this, you would normally type I for the search string and **we** for the replacement string, and fully expect WordPerfect to make the corrections. However, because your search string contains an uppercase letter, WordPerfect replaces every "I" with We, and changes phrases such as "Still, I want" to "Still, We want" (with "we" capitalized, mistakenly.)

Things get worse if you try to change a capitalized word to lowercase, because WordPerfect won't make the replacements. Worse yet, it won't even tell you that it hasn't made the replacements! For example, suppose you entered **Winter** instead of winter throughout a document. If you do a Replace operation with "Winter" as the search string and "winter" as the replacement string, WordPerfect will go merrily along, but leave "Winter" intact in each case.

To eliminate these problems, you should replace each uppercase string by using Search, rather than Replace. That is, make WordPerfect find the string you want to replace, then delete the entire string (or just the capitalized letter in it) and type the replacement. Of course, this involves doing a Search operation for each occurrence. In Chapter 9, we discuss how to use something called *macros* to automate the replacement procedure.

Wildcard Searches

Sometimes you may want to search for any of several similarly spelled words. You can do this by entering Ctrl-X in the search string for each character that may differ from one occurrence to another. To WordPerfect, Ctrl-X (shown as ^X) is a *wildcard* character; it acts as shorthand for any single character. You may compare it with the Joker in popular card games, a free number in Bingo, or a blank tile in Scrabble.

For example, to find every mention of dates in the 1970s, you could perform a Search command and enter **197^X** as the search string. This makes WordPerfect stop on 1970, 1971, 1972, and so on.

You cannot enter ^X as the first character in a search string, but you can put it anywhere else. You can even put several ^Xs in a search string. For example, you could use **19-^X^X-3657** to find all mentions of part numbers that start with 19 and end with 3657.

You can also include ^Xs in the -> *Srch:* string of a Replace command, but not in its *Replace with:* string. Of course, if you use them, you should always answer *Yes* to *w/Confirm?*.

Abbreviations

Replace also allows you to use abbreviations when typing a document. This is like the common practice in note-taking of jotting down UN for United Nations or DoD for United States Department of Defense.

For example, if you are writing a report on European sales, you may simply type UK for United Kingdom, WG (West Germany) for Federal Republic of Germany, and EEC for European Economic Community. Then, when you have finished, do replace operations to expand the abbreviations. Be sure that your abbreviations are distinct (note, for instance, that you will find US in USSR) and do not conflict with each other (such as using UN for United Nations and University of Nebraska).

Replace has the advantage of making WordPerfect—not *you*—expand the abbreviations.

WINDOWS

WordPerfect lets you divide the screen into two areas, or *windows*. Each can display a different document. Once you have set up the second window, you can work in either of them.

Why would you want to use two windows? You can, for example, do the following:

1. Examine previous correspondence, a contract, or other document while writing a letter. You may even want to copy sections from that document.
2. Look back at an earlier report to be sure you are using the same format, terminology, or spelling.
3. Examine an outline while you write, and check off sections as you finish them.
4. Take figures, tables, or terminology from old versions of a document, partial or extended versions, or standard forms. Thus, you could use part of last year's report or the last project's contract in a new report or contract. You could also combine weekly reports into a monthly report or excerpt a brief synopsis from a complete project report.

WordPerfect's main work area is itself a window (#1, as indicated by the *Doc 1* on the status line). WordPerfect will label the second window *Doc 2*.

Opening a Window

To open the second window, press Ctrl-F3 for Screen. When the following menu appears:

```
0 Rewrite; 1 Window; 2 Line Draw; 3 Ctrl/Alt keys;
4 Colors; 5 Auto Rewrite: 0
```

type 1 for Window. This produces the prompt

Lines in this Window: 24

Now, press the up- or down-arrow key until a lighted tab ruler appears. Note that as you move the tab ruler, the *# Lines* value increases. Continue pressing the arrow keys until the bottom window is the size you want; then press Enter.

Switching Between Windows

Although the second window is open, the first window is still active. To switch to the second window (i.e., make it active), press Shift-F3 for Switch. The cursor moves to the top of the second window. Now you can create a new document or retrieve an existing one. When you want to switch back to the first window, press Shift-F3 (Switch) again.

Note that the windows are independent. Once you Retrieve a document into a window, it is a separate entity. You can work on it without affecting the document in the other window.

Operating on Windows

WordPerfect treats the active window just like the full screen. You can edit, move the cursor, retrieve or save a document, issue commands, and so on.

Moving Text Between Windows

The only special part of moving text to another window is that you must remember to switch windows. That is, you go through the usual process using the Move command to select the text and either Cut or Copy it. You must then press Shift-F3 to switch windows. Now you can finish the task by moving the cursor to where you want the text and doing another Move to paste it.

Closing a Window

To close a window, switch to the other window, then press Shift-F3 to obtain the Screen menu and select *Window*. When the *# Lines in this Window* message appears, enter **25**. The tab ruler and window text disappear.

Closing does not affect the contents of a window; it simply makes WordPerfect take the window off the screen. You can still reach a closed window with Switch. Thus, if you do an Exit command from either window, WordPerfect will display the Save and Exit prompts for each document, Doc 1 and Doc 2.

As you have seen, WordPerfect's window feature is handy for referring to one document while you work on another one, and for copying text between documents. If, however, you just want to look at parts of a different document (or a different part of this one), you don't have to use a window.

VIEWING DOCUMENTS

The List Files menu has a *Look* option that lets you view any document on the data disk, including the one you're working on. With it, you can, for example, check a table, chart, or quotation while preparing a description of it. You can also use it to look back at an earlier part of a report, to avoid repetitions and (worse) contradictions. Thus, Look gives you quick access to a document without going to all the bother of loading it into memory.

To look at a document, press F5 for List Files. When the list appears, use the arrow keys to highlight the document, then type **6** for Look. Once the document appears on the screen, you can use the down-arrow key to move down the screen, + (Screen Down) on the numeric keypad to reach the bottom line on the screen, or PgDn to reach the next page. Pressing any other key makes the file list reappear.

REFORMATTING DOCUMENTS

Sometimes you must reformat an entire document. For example, you may have double spaced a report (so you could edit it easily), but want to print the final version single-spaced. Reformatting a document is easiest if you entered it using WordPerfect's automatic format settings. Then you simply move the cursor to the beginning of the document (by pressing Home twice and then up-arrow), and do one or more Line Format commands to specify your new settings.

It's also easy to reformat a document that uses the same format settings throughout. Move the cursor to the beginning of the document and give a Reveal Codes (Alt-F3) command. The Reveal Codes display shows a [Tab Set:], [Margin Set:], or [Spacing Set:] code if you set the tabs, margins, or line spacing. To change one of these values, delete its code by moving the cursor just ahead of it and pressing Del—or just beyond it and pressing Backspace. Then press Enter to get back to editing, and give a Line Format command to obtain the settings you want. WordPerfect makes the change throughout the document automatically.

Things get a little trickier if you want to reformat a document that includes format changes. In that case, you must locate each format code you want to change, delete the code, and perform a Line Format command that provides the settings you want. Suppose, for example, that you have a double-spaced report that includes single-spaced tables, and you want everything single-spaced.

Single Spacing a Double-Spaced Document

To single space a double-spaced document, move the cursor to the beginning of the document and use Reveal Codes to delete the [Spacing Set:2] code. This makes WordPerfect revert to its default, single spacing, which means it will single space everything up to the next [Spacing Set:] code.

At this point, of course, you could move through the document looking for where double-spacing begins again and delete the code. But why go to the trouble? Let WordPerfect find each code and delete it for you! With the cursor at the beginning of the document, you can find the next [Spacing Set:] code by doing the following:

1. Press Alt-F2 to start a Replace operation and type **n** when WordPerfect asks *w/Confirm? (Y/N) N*.
2. When the *-> Srch:* prompt appears, press Shift-F8 to do a Line Format command.
3. When the Line Format menu appears, type **4** for Spacing ([Spacing Set] appears in the response field); then press F2.
4. When the *Replace with:* prompt appears, press F2 to start replacing. (Pressing F2 here tells WordPerfect to replace each [Spacing Set:] code with nothing. In other words, it tells WordPerfect to delete the code.)

WordPerfect searches through your entire document, and deletes spacing codes as it goes. When it finishes, the document appears in single-spaced form.

Deleting Other Codes

You can also use replace operations to locate and delete other codes in a document. For example, you can eliminate bold print, centering, or underlining by pressing F6, Shift-F6, or F8 in response to the *-> Srch:* prompt. Furthermore, you can eliminate selected occurrences of these formats by typing **y** in response to the *w/Confirm? (Y/N) N* prompt.

QUESTIONS AND ANSWERS

Question: I need the same table headings several times in a report. How can I avoid retyping them?

Answer: Highlight the headings in Block mode; then give WordPerfect a Move command and choose the Copy Block option. Next move the cursor to each place you want the headings, give another Move command, and choose Text from the Move/Retrieve menu. WordPerfect will keep the headings until you cut or copy something else.

Question: I searched for a phrase that I know is in my report, but WordPerfect couldn't find it. Why not?

Answer: The most likely reason is that you had the cursor past where the phrase occurred and did a Search Forward, or ahead of the phrase and did a Search Backward. Try searching from the beginning of the report. Also check the spelling; if you misspelled something, WordPerfect surely won't find the phrase.

Question: I just finished my monthly sales report when the Northwest sales office called with some corrections. How can I find all the places where I might have mentioned their figures?

Answer: Move the cursor to the beginning of the report, then start a Search operation. Next enter **Northwest** and press F2 to begin the search. WordPerfect will stop the first time it finds *Northwest*. To find the next occurrence, press F2 twice. If something needs changing, move the cursor to it and make the changes, and then press F2 twice to resume the search.

Question: I misspelled "principle" as "principal" throughout a term paper. How can I correct it?

Answer: Move the cursor to the beginning of the document and do a Replace operation. Enter **principal** for -> *Srch:* and **principle** for *Replace with:*. Be sure you don't put a space after either entry, so WordPerfect will correct such variations as "principals" and will find occurrences at the ends of sentences.

Question: Our company's statement of qualifications always refers to us as "Smith, Brown, Jones, and Associates, Inc." Unfortunately, after a minor argument and a small lawsuit, Brown left and is now our chief competitor. How do I change the name to "Smith, Jones, and Associates, Inc." and make sure Brown isn't mentioned anywhere?

Answer: You can remove Brown from the company name by doing a Replace. Use *Smith, Brown* as the search string and *Smith* (no comma) as the replacement. Then search the entire statement for *Brown* and change the text as required. I would even do a final search for *Brown* just to make sure I hadn't missed any mentions. Better to be safe and expend a few keystrokes and some computer time than to worry.

HINTS AND WARNINGS

1. Watch the distinction between moving and copying text. With the Move command, selecting *Cut* starts a move operation, which deletes text from its old position; selecting Copy starts a copy operation, which leaves the original as it was.

2. When performing a move or copy operation, remember that WordPerfect does not preserve the original format. You must manually correct it at the destination by doing a Line Format command before and after the moved material.

3. When moving text, insert it at its destination immediately. If the power goes off or you absent-mindedly switch the computer off, you will lose it. If the telephone rings or a visitor drops in, finish moving the text before acknowledging the interruption. Otherwise, you may not remember what you were doing when you return to it.

4. Remember that WordPerfect holds anything you move or copy until you do another Move operation. You can insert moved or copied material over and over by selecting *Text* from the Move/Retrieve menu.

5. The Move command is handy for deleting a sentence, paragraph, or page. Simply select the unit and Cut it. Since the unit remains in memory until you do another Cut or Copy, you can undelete it by giving WordPerfect another Move and choosing *Text*.

6. Be careful when you do a Replace with the *w/Confirm?* option set to *N* for global replacement. WordPerfect does not indicate what it replaced or how many replacements it made. If you aren't absolutely sure you want to make the replacement each time, use *Y* for selective replacement. This is may take some time, but it can avoid errors that are almost impossible to find.
7. Note that Search can go forward or backward, while Replace always goes forward.
8. WordPerfect's Replace command does not let you replace an uppercase word or phrase with a lowercase one. To do this, perform a Search-delete-enter procedure rather than a Replace operation.
9. You can cancel a move, copy, search, or selective replace operation at any time by pressing F1.
10. To copy material from one part of a document to another, you can open a window and retrieve the current document into it; then do the copy operation. Be careful doing this, however, because when you Exit, WordPerfect will ask if you want to save both windows. Save the first window (Doc 1), but not the second (Doc 2).

KEY POINT SUMMARY

Table 6-1 summarizes the editing keys we introduced.

1. To move a sentence, paragraph, or page, put the cursor anywhere in it and press Ctrl-F4 for *Move*; then select the text unit from the Move/Retrieve menu and Cut from the Cut/Copy menu. Next, move the cursor to the new location and press Ctrl-F4 again. This time, select *Text* from the menu.
2. To copy a sentence, paragraph, or page, use the same procedure as for moving one, but select *Copy* from the Cut/Copy menu.
3. Moving or copying a block of text requires a similar procedure to the ones we just mentioned, but begin by pressing Alt-F4 to put WordPerfect in Block mode, then Ctrl-F4 for Move. When the menu appears, select *Cut Block* or *Copy Block*.

Table 6-1. Keys Introduced in Chapter 6.

Key(s)	Function
F2	Search forward
Alt-F2	Replace
Shift-F2	Search backward
Ctrl-F3	Screen
Shift-F3	Switch to other window
Ctrl-F4	Move (or copy) a sentence, paragraph, page, block, or column
Ctrl-X	Wildcard character in a search string

4. To move or copy a column of text or numbers, start as you would for a block (i.e., obtain Block mode and highlight the column), but when the Move/Retrieve menu appears, select *Cut/Copy Column.* To paste the column, do another move and select *Column* from the Move/Retrieve menu.

5. Besides ordinary text, WordPerfect can insert, delete, move, or copy columns of text or numbers that you have entered using tabs.

6. To insert a column, set a tab for it and move the remaining tabs right. Then put the cursor where you want the insertion and enter the new data items. Press Tab at the end of each one, to move the existing material right.

7. To delete a column, move the cursor to the beginning of it and press Alt-F4 to put WordPerfect in Block mode. Then move the cursor to the last character in the column and press Ctrl-F4 to do a Move. Select *Cut/Copy Column* from the menu and then *Cut* from the Cut/Copy menu.

8. To move a column, *Cut* it using the procedure we just gave for deleting one; then move the cursor to where you want the column and press Ctrl-F4 for Move. When the Move/Retrieve menu appears, select *Column.* Copying a column is the same as moving one, except you select *Copy* instead of *Cut.*

9. WordPerfect can search a document for a specified *string* (a sequence of characters). To begin, press F2 to search forward or Shift-F2 to search backward. When WordPerfect displays its *-> Srch:* or *<- Srch:* prompt, enter the search string and press F2. Search strings starting with a capital letter will only find occurrences that start with a capital letter; lowercase search strings will find every occurrence.

10. WordPerfect can also search a document for a string and replace it with another of your choice. To start a replace, press Alt-F2.

11. At the beginning of a Replace operation, WordPerfect displays *w/Confirm? (Y/N) N.* *N* makes it replace every occurrence of the search string automatically, while *Y* makes it stop each time and ask whether you want to replace the occurrence. Pressing F1 cancels the Replace operation.

12. The Replace operation produces two more prompts. For *-> Srch:*, type the search string and press F2; for *Replace with:*, type the replacement string and press F2 again.

13. Both Search and Replace lets you include wildcard characters in the search string. This allows you to search for any of several similarly spelled words. To enter a wildcard character, press Ctrl-X where it is to appear.

14. Replace can be handy for expanding abbreviations in your document.

15. WordPerfect can display two documents at once in separate areas called *windows.*

16. To create (or *open*) a window, press Ctrl-F3 for *Screen*; then select *Window* from the menu. Press the up- or down-arrow key until the tab ruler appears, and continue pressing it until the window at the bottom is the size you want.

17. WordPerfect operates only on the document in the *active* window. To switch windows, press Shift-F3 for Switch.

18. Once the second window is active, you can create a new document in it or

retrieve an existing document from disk. You can then move or copy material between the windows.

19. To close a window, give WordPerfect an Exit command.

20. To view a disk document, do a List Files (F5) command, highlight the document you want, and select *Look*. When the document appears, use the down-arrow key to move down the screen, + (Screen Down) on the numeric key-pad to reach the bottom line on the screen, or PgDn to reach the next page. Pressing any other key makes the file list reappear.

21. To reformat a document, set up the format you want at the beginning of it; then do Replace operations in which you search for other format codes and replace them with nothing (i.e., delete them).

Chapter 7

Special Features

If your document is long, you should prepare an outline before starting to work on it. You may also want to number the section titles as they'll be numbered in the document. Section numbering is especially common for term papers, research reports, and technical specifications and manuals. Further, you may want to number paragraphs as you enter them; this is often required for legal contracts.

Normally, the writer must supply the numbers and keep track of them—an annoying job at best. It becomes even more tedious if he or she adds or deletes a subsection, because that changes the numbering on all subsequent subsections. WordPerfect can help eliminate these problems, by inserting the numbers automatically. It provides up to seven levels of numbering and three different styles: Paragraph, Outline, and Legal. The numbers they produce are of these forms:

Paragraph	1. a. i. (1) (a) (i) 1)
Outline	I. A. 1. a. (1) (a) 1)
Legal	1., 1.1, 2, 2.1, etc.

Besides numbering, WordPerfect has several other special features that can speed up your work. It can:

- Generate tables of contents, indexes, and lists
- Perform mathematical calculations on rows and columns of numbers
- Draw lines and boxes, to create bar charts or to simply dress up material

PREPARING OUTLINES

When preparing an outline, you can make WordPerfect number the section titles before or after you enter them. In doing this, WordPerfect works much as you would. That is, you enter first-level (section or chapter) titles at the left-hand margin, indent second-level (subsection) titles one tab stop, indent third-level (sub-subsection) titles two tab stops, and so on. However, each time you start a new line or press Tab, WordPerfect automatically inserts the next number for that level. You needn't type the numbers or remember which one comes next, as you do when you prepare an outline on a typewriter.

Once WordPerfect is in its Outline Number mode, two different keys make it produce a section number:

- Pressing Enter makes it insert a first-level number (e.g., I, II, III) at the beginning of the next line
- Pressing *Tab* makes it move to the next tab stop and insert the next level number there.

WordPerfect can produce up to seven levels of numbering. Its normal style uses these starting numbers at the respective levels:

I. A. 1. a. (1) (a) i)

Using the Outline Number Feature

To make WordPerfect number an outline, enter a heading (if you want one), and then proceed as follows:

1. Set tabs for the section numbers and the titles that follow them.
2. Press Alt-F5 for Mark Text. This produces the following menu:

1 Outline; 2 Para #; 3 Redline; 4 Remove; 5 Index;
6 Define; 7 Generate: 0

3. Type 1 to select Outline. WordPerfect shows *Outline* at the bottom of the screen.
4. Press Enter to reach the line where the outline should start. Enter makes WordPerfect display *I.* at the left margin. (To put more lines between the title and the outline, continue pressing Enter.)
5. To reach the place where the title starts, press Indent (F4) or the space bar.

(You wouldn't want to press Tab here, because that would make WordPerfect advance to the next numbering level.)

6. Type the section title, then press Enter. WordPerfect inserts *II.* the next first-level number.
7. Now you have two choices:

- To produce another first-level title, enter it as described in steps 4 and 5.
- To produce a second-level title, press Tab.

As we mentioned earlier, every time you press Tab, WordPerfect advances to the next numbering level. Thus, pressing Tab once from the left margin sets up a second-level title, pressing it twice sets up a third-level title, and so on.

To turn the Outline Number feature off, do another Mark Text command and select *Outline* again.

A Sample Outline

Figure 7-1 shows an outline that appears in the WordPerfect manual. Here, the first-level titles (e.g., *I. Big Game Reserve*) are entered at the left margin, second-level titles (e.g., *A. Permits*) are at the first tab stop, and third-level titles (e.g., *1. Animals*) are at the second tab stop.

EDITING OUTLINES

Unless your document is simple and straightforward, you will probably spend quite a bit of time preparing an outline for it. Typically, you create a preliminary outline, with perhaps only the first- and second-level titles. Then you survey this first attempt and decide what to change.

Often, you want to make the outline more detailed, by inserting new section or subsection titles. You may also want to delete titles or change their priority; say, change a second-level title to first level, or vice versa. Finally, you may want to change the order of certain sections, by moving them from one part of the outline to another.

Of course, all of these operations affect the numbering within the outline. With a typewriter, they would require you to spend hours either cutting and pasting or retyping. With WordPerfect on a computer, they take only seconds. And better yet, WordPerfect renumbers everything automatically to reflect the changes!

Inserting

To insert an entry into an outline, move the cursor to the end of the line that is to precede the insertion; then start as usual—by selecting Mark Text's Outline option. Press Enter to start a new line and Tab to indent to the level you want. Finally, type your insertion—but *don't* press Enter after it unless you want to in-

```
    I.  Big Game Reserve

        A.    Permits
              1.   Animals
              2.   Hunting Hours
              3.   Tags
              4.   Annual Totals

        B.    Big Game Hunts and Conservation
              1.   Permit Reduction
              2.   Legal Age
              3.   Deer and Elk Exceptions

   II.  Campgrounds

  III.  Wilderness Mountain Area

   IV.  Lone Pine Reserve
```

Fig. 7-1. A sample outline.

sert another entry. WordPerfect renumbers as you move the cursor down the screen or leave Outline mode.

Deleting

You can delete an outline entry just as you delete ordinary text; you don't even have to put WordPerfect into Outline mode. When the entry disappears, WordPerfect closes the gap and renumbers to reflect the deletion.

Changing Levels

As you know, WordPerfect numbers each outline entry based on how many tab stops you indented it. The amount of indentation determines the entry's level, and thus its number.

Fortunately, if you indent too much or too little, and enter a title at the wrong level, you can easily correct it. Simply move the cursor to the beginning of the number and press Backspace or Tab once for each level you want to raise or lower the entry. For example, to change a third-level title to first-level, move the cursor to its number and press Backspace twice. When you move the cursor down the screen, WordPerfect renumbers every entry to reflect the level change.

Moving and Copying

Once you prepare an outline using Outline mode, WordPerfect keeps track of the numbering. Thus, if you move or copy numbered titles using the standard techniques, WordPerfect corrects the affected numbers automatically. Generally, you move titles to change the order of the document, and copy them as a basis for creating similar entries.

NUMBERING PARAGRAPHS

WordPerfect's Paragraph Number feature can number paragraphs, titles, and lists in a document. To make it do this, however, you must explicitly tell it to insert a paragraph number *every* time you want one. WordPerfect does not insert numbers automatically, as it does for outlines.

Using the Paragraph Number Feature

To start numbering paragraphs, move the cursor to where you want the first number and press Alt-F5 for Mark Text. When the Mark Text menu appears, type 2 to select *Para #*. This produces the prompt

Paragraph Level (ENTER for automatic):

WordPerfect is waiting for you to tell it which of two types of numbers you want, *automatic* or *fixed*.

Automatic Numbers and Fixed Numbers

With automatic paragraph numbering, WordPerfect inserts the appropriate level for the tab position the cursor is currently on. That is, it inserts a first-level number at the first tab position, a second-level number at the second, and so on. By contrast, fixed paragraph numbering lets you tell WordPerfect which level of number to insert, regardless of which tab position the cursor is at. For example, you can make it insert a fourth-level number at the first tab position.

In short, there are three ways to respond to the *Paragraph Level* prompt:

- To insert an automatic number, press Enter. WordPerfect uses the level that reflects how many times you pressed Tab *before* requesting the number.
- To insert a fixed number, enter a number between 1 and 7. WordPerfect inserts the next number for that particular level.
- To return to editing without inserting a number, press F1.

When should you use fixed paragraph numbers instead of automatic ones?

In general, use fixed numbers if you want a specific level number, regardless of which tab position the cursor is on, or if you want a numbered title centered and the number would fall between two tabs. For any other application, use automatic numbers.

I suppose most people can use fixed paragraph numbers exclusively. Only those who must prepare complex technical documents such as specifications must revert to automatic numbers.

EDITING NUMBERED TEXT

Sometimes you must insert, delete, move, or copy numbered paragraphs within a document. You may also want to change the priority of a paragraph; say, change a third-level number to first level. As with an outline, WordPerfect recognizes your change and renumbers automatically.

You can delete, move, or copy a numbered paragraph as you would regular unnumbered text; WordPerfect will change the numbers as appropriate. Inserting or changing levels, however, requires techniques we have not yet discussed.

Inserting

To insert a new numbered paragraph, move the cursor to the end of the line that is to precede your insertion and press Enter to start a new line. Then select Mark Text's *Para #* option and insert the number and then the paragraph in the usual way.

Changing Levels

If you have inserted a number at the wrong level (say, you inserted a third-level number when you meant to use second-level) or simply want to raise or lower the priority of a paragraph, you can easily make WordPerfect change the paragraph's number. Simply delete the number and then insert a new one. That is, move the cursor to the number and press Del, or move it just past the number and press Backspace. When WordPerfect displays

Delete [Par#]? (Y/N) N

type y. The number disappears. To insert the new number, give another Mark Text command, select *Para #*, and respond to the prompt as usual (by selecting automatic or fixed numbering).

SWITCHING NUMBERING STYLES

WordPerfect uses the Outline style of numbering automatically, but you can make it switch to Paragraph, Legal, or a style of your own design at any time. To switch numbering styles, give a Mark Text command and type **6** for *Define*. When the *Text Marking Definition* menu appears (see Fig. 7-2), type **7** for Paragraph/Outline Numbering.

When the Paragraph Numbering Definition menu appears, type **1** for Paragraph Style, **2** for Outline Style, **3** for Legal Style, or **4** for Other (to create a style of your own). Then start entering your outline or numbered paragraphs as usual.

For example, if you had switched to Paragraph Style before entering our sample outline, WordPerfect would have numbered the beginning of the outline like this:

1. Big Game Reserve

   a. Permits
     i. Animals

Similarly, switching to Legal Style would produce:

1. Big Game Reserve

   1.1. Permits
     1.1.0.1 Animals

You can even switch numbering styles *after* finishing a project. Simply move the cursor to where numbering starts and give a Reveal Codes command. When the Reveal Codes display appears, move the cursor just past the [Par#Def] code (that's where you defined the style) and press Backspace to delete it. Then press

---

Text Marking Definition

1 - List 1
2 - List 2
3 - List 3
4 - List 4
5 - List 5
6 - Table of Contents
7 - Paragraph/Outline Numbering
8 - Index

Fig. 7-2. The Text Marking Definition menu.

Enter to leave Reveal Codes. Finally, use Mark Text command's Define option to specify the new style. WordPerfect instantly renumbers everything using the new style.

You can also use the Define option to select the *same* numbering style. This is necessary when you want WordPerfect to start numbering back at 1.

Restarting the Numbering

Once WordPerfect starts numbering text or an outline, it continues using that sequence until you tell it to stop. This causes problems if, for example, you prepare an outline, and then start a new page and begin entering regular text. WordPerfect will simply resume numbering where it left off. If the last title in your outline is numbered V., it will number the first section title in your text VI.

Similarly, if your document contains two numbered lists, WordPerfect assumes you want the numbers on the second list to start where the first list ended; it treats the second list as a continuation of the first one. To make it start renumbering from 1 (or I), use the Mark Text command's Define option and select your current style again.

TABLES OF CONTENTS

WordPerfect can also generate a table of contents if you tell it what to include. You can specify any of five different numbering styles, including no page numbers, a page number following each entry, or page numbers at the right-hand margin.

Building a Table of Contents

To build a table of contents, you must tell WordPerfect what to include. Do this as follows:

1. Move the cursor to the beginning of the first section title you want to include (or to its number, if it has one), and put WordPerfect in Block mode.
2. Press End to select the rest of the line.
3. Press Alt-F5 to give a Mark Text command. WordPerfect displays

```
Mark for 1 Table of Contents; 2 List; 3 Redline;
4 Strikeout; 5 Index: 0
```

4. Type 1 to select Table of Contents.
5. When WordPerfect shows *ToC Level:*, enter a number between 1 and 5. The

number you enter specifies the level of this particular title; it tells WordPerfect how much to indent the title in the table of contents. Entering **1** positions the title at the left margin, entering **2** indents it one tab stop, and so on.

Repeat these steps for each title you want included in the table of contents. When you finish, move the cursor to where the table of contents belongs (generally, it follows the title page) and start a new page with Ctrl-Enter. Then enter a heading, if you want one, and set tabs for the table. Now you must tell WordPerfect which format or numbering style to use.

Defining the Numbering Style

WordPerfect can generate a table of contents in any of five numbering styles. They are:

1. No page numbers (only numbers and titles)
2. Page numbers follow entries
3. Page numbers follow entries, but are enclosed in parentheses. For example, if the "Major Products" entry is on page 43, this option would produce

   Major Products (43)

4. Flush right pages numbers; that is, numbers are aligned along the right-hand margin.
5. Flush right page numbers with leaders; WordPerfect inserts periods between the end of the title and the page number.

To select the style, begin by pressing Alt-F5 and typing **6** for Define. When the Marking Text Definition menu appears, type **6** for Table of Contents. WordPerfect displays its Table of Contents Definition menu (Fig. 7-3).

The prompt at the top is asking how many levels of indentation you want in your table of contents. To put every entry at the left-hand margin, type **1**; otherwise, type a number between **2** and **5**.

WordPerfect then shows the prompt *Display last level in wrapped format? (Y/N) N*. Normally, type **n** to put each entry on a separate line. If you type **y**, it will place entries of the last (highest-numbered) level on the same line, and separate them with semicolons.

WordPerfect next needs to know which Page Number Position option you want. It assumes you want *Flush Right Page Numbers with Leaders*, and displays *5* on as many "Level" lines as you specified. If you really want that format, press Enter until the menu disappears; otherwise, choose a different numbering option by typing its number on each "Level" line. When your document reappears, you can generate the table of contents.

Table of Contents Definition

Number of levels in table of contents (1-5): 0

                           Page Number Position
Level 1
Level 2
Level 3
Level 4
Level 5

Page Number Position
1 - No Page Numbers
2 - Page Numbers Follow Entries
3 - (Page Numbers) Follow Entries
4 - Flush Right Page Numbers
5 - Flush Right Numbers with Leaders

Fig. 7-3. The Table of Contents Definition menu.

Generating a Table of Contents

To make WordPerfect generate the table of contents, obtain the Mark Text menu (Alt-F5) and select *Generate*. When the screen shows

Have you deleted your old Table of Contents, Lists and Index? (Y/N) N

type **y**. (We'll discuss the *N* option shortly.)

Finally, WordPerfect begins creating the table of contents, and displays

Generation in progress. Counter: *n*

at the bottom of the screen. When it finishes, your table of contents appears.

Entries in the table of contents will be indented according to their level numbers. Each however, will have the same format as in the document; that is, bold text will be bold in the table, underlined text will be underlined, and so on. You may want to edit the table of contents to remove these print formats.

INDEXES

You can also make WordPerfect generate an index for your document, based on words or phrases you specify. Generating an index involves the same three procedures you use to generate a table of contents. That is, *build* the index by selecting entries, *define* the numbering style, then *generate* the index.

Headings and Subheadings

In addition to regular index entries or *headings*, WordPerfect also lets you define *subheadings*; that is, entries that fall under a general heading. For example, the index for a financial report may include

Sales
   and commission record 271
   to accounts receivables 167
   to cash 180
   to fixed assets 185
   to inventories 190

Here, "Sales" is a heading and the indented lines are subheadings.

Building an Index

You can build an index by selecting either phrases or individual words. *To select a phrase*, move the cursor to the beginning of it and put WordPerfect in Block mode. Then highlight the phrase by pressing either the right-arrow key to select characters or Ctrl and right-arrow to select words. *To select a specific word*, simply move the cursor to it. Either way, proceed as follows:

1. Press Alt-F5 to give a Mark Text command.
2. When the menu appears, type **5** to select Index. WordPerfect shows *Index Heading:* and the word or phrase you selected.
3. Now you can do either of two things:

   • To make the entry a heading, press Enter. When the prompt *Subheading:* appears at the bottom of the screen, enter a subheading (if you want one); then press Enter.
   • To make the entry a subheading, type a heading, and then press Enter.

When *Subheading:* and your entry appear at the bottom of the screen, press Enter.

Repeat these steps for each word or phrase you want included in the index. When you finish, move the cursor to the end of your document (press Home twice and then down-arrow) and start a new page (Ctrl-Enter). Then set tabs for the index and enter a heading, if you want one. Now you must tell WordPerfect which numbering style to use.

Defining the Numbering Style

To create an index, WordPerfect can use any of the five numbering styles it provides for tables of contents. To select the style, begin by pressing Alt-F5 and typing **6** for Define. When the Marking Text Definition menu appears, type **8** for Index. WordPerfect displays its *Index Definition* menu. This is the same as the bottom part of the Table of Contents Definition menu; it simply lists the available numbering styles. Select the style you want by typing its number.

Generating an Index

To make WordPerfect generate the index, obtain the Mark Text menu (Alt-F5) and select *Generate*. When the screen shows

Have you deleted your old Table of Contents, Lists and Index? (Y/N) N

type y. WordPerfect begins creating the index, and displays

Generation in progress. Counter: *n*

at the bottom of the screen. When it finishes, the index appears.

WordPerfect puts headings at the left-hand margin and indents subheadings. It also produces both headings and subheadings in alphabetical order, thereby saving you the trouble of rearranging them. As with a table of contents, each index entry will have the same form as in the document (e.g., bold text will be bold in the index). As before, you may want to edit the index to remove these print formats.

LISTS

In addition to a table of contents and index, WordPerfect can also produce up to five different lists, based on words or phrases you specify. This is handy for summarizing page numbers for figures, illustrations, and tables in a document.

Creating a list involves the same three procedures you use to generate a table of contents or an index. That is, *build* the list by selecting entries, *define* the numbering style, and then *generate* the list.

Building a List

To build a list, you must tell WordPerfect what to include. To begin, move the cursor to the beginning of the word or phrase you want and put WordPerfect in Block mode. Then highlight the text by either pressing the right-arrow key to select characters or pressing Ctrl and right-arrow to select words. With that done, proceed as follows:

1. Press Alt-F5 to give a Mark Text command. WordPerfect displays

Mark for 1 Table of Contents; 2 List; 3 Redline;
4 Strikeout; 5 Index: 0

2. Type **2** to select List.
3. When WordPerfect shows *List #:*, enter a number between 1 and 5, to indicate the list you want to create.

Repeat these steps for each word or phrase you want included in the list. When you finish, move the cursor to where the list should start and enter a heading if you want one. Now you must tell WordPerfect which numbering style to use.

Defining the Numbering Style

To create a list, WordPerfect can use any of the five numbering styles it provides for tables of contents and indexes. To select the style, begin by pressing Alt-F5 and typing **6** for Define. When the Marking Text Definition menu appears, type a number between 1 and 5, to identify your list. WordPerfect displays its

List Definition menu. This is the same as the Index Definition menu; it simply lists the available numbering styles. Select the style you want by typing its number.

Generating a List

To make WordPerfect generate the list, obtain the Mark Text menu (Alt-F5) and select *Generate*. When the screen shows

Have you deleted your old Table of Contents, Lists and Index? (Y/N) N

type **y**. WordPerfect begins creating the list, and displays

Generation in progress. Counter: *n*

at the bottom of the screen. When it finishes, the list appears.

WordPerfect puts each list entry at the left-hand margin. It also arranges them in ascending order by page number, but (unfortunately) does not sort them alphabetically; for any given page number, WordPerfect simply lists the entries in the order you entered them. (In Chapter 8, we describe how to sort lists.)

As with a table of contents or index, each list entry has the same form as in the document (e.g., bold text is bold in the index). As before, you may want to edit the list to remove these print formats.

UPDATING TABLES OF CONTENTS, INDEXES, AND LISTS

Usually you generate the table of contents, index, and lists when you finish a document, so those parts remain unchanged thereafter. If, however, you are subject to higher authority (who isn't?), someone may suggest—or demand—changes that alter the final form. If these changes only affect a few words, you can simply make the revisions and reprint the document. But if they affect page numbering or require adding or deleting references, you must update the document.

To *add* entries to a table of contents, index, or list, perform the procedures we just described for building one.

To *remove* entries from a table of contents, index or list, you must either delete their text or delete the invisible code that identifies them as entries. WordPerfect marks each table of contents entry by placing a code of the form *[Mark:ToC,n]* ahead of it and *[EndMark:ToC,n]* after it; in each case, the *n* indicates the table of contents level. Similarly, it encloses each list entry with codes of the form *[Mark:List,n]* and *[EndMark:List,n]*, where *n* is the list number. Finally, WordPerfect marks each index entry by preceding it with a code of the form *[Index:text]*, where *text* is the text of the entry.

Therefore, to remove an entry from a table of contents or list, use Reveal Codes (Alt-F3) to locate the beginning Mark code and press Del or Backspace to delete it (WordPerfect deletes the corresponding EndMark code automatically). To remove an entry from an index, use Reveal Codes to locate the Index code and Del or Backspace to delete it.

Once you have altered the contents of a table of contents, index, or list, you must produce an updated version of it. To do this, select *Generate* from the menu, but when WordPerfect asks *Have you deleted your old Table of Contents, Lists, and Index?*, type n. This makes WordPerfect highlight the existing table, index, or list and show *Delete Block? (Y/N) N*; type y to delete it. Now that the old unit is gone, WordPerfect generates a new one.

MATHEMATICAL OPERATIONS

WordPerfect can perform math operations on numeric tables. For example, it can add a column of numbers to produce a *subtotal*. It can then add subtotals to produce a *total* and add totals to produce a *grand total*. WordPerfect can also perform calculations on the rows in a table. It can add, subtract, multiply, or divide rows of numbers based on simple formulas that you enter.

WordPerfect can handle up to 24 columns at a time. Columns are located at tab stops. That is, column A is at the first tab stop, column B is at the second tab stop, and so on. The text at the left-hand margin can only be used to label the rows; it is not counted as a column.

Instead of entering numbers in columns, you can enter calculation formulas or text, or you can make WordPerfect produce totals and grand totals in separate columns. How WordPerfect treats a column depends on whether you define its type as Numeric, Calculation, Text, or Total.

Adding Columns

WordPerfect is initially set up to add columns, so that's the easiest kind of operation to do. To add columns, you must set up tabs for them, turn on the Math feature, enter the numbers, perform the addition, and then turn Math off. The procedure is:

1. For each column, set a tab where you want the decimal point to appear.

2. Press Alt and F7 to give a Math/Columns command. WordPerfect shows this Math Definition menu:

1 Math On; 2 Math Def; 3 Column On/Off; 4 Column Def: 0

To just add columns vertically, skip steps 3 and 4.

3. Type **2** for Math Def. WordPerfect displays a Math Definition screen (see Fig. 7-4).

For each of the 24 possible columns (A - X), the Math Definition screen lists the type of column and tells how it intends to display answers. Unless you change these parameters, WordPerfect will make all columns Numeric and display answers with two digits to the right of the decimal point, with

```
Math Definition      Use Arrow keys to position cursor

Columns              A  B  C  D  E  F  G  H  I  J  K  L  M  N  O  P  Q  R  S  T  U  V  W  X

Type                 2  2  2  2  2  2  2  2  2  2  2  2  2  2  2  2  2  2  2  2  2  2  2  2

Negative Numbers     (  (  (  (  (  (  (  (  (  (  (  (  (  (  (  (  (  (  (  (  (  (  (  (

# of digits to       2  2  2  2  2  2  2  2  2  2  2  2  2  2  2  2  2  2  2  2  2  2  2  2
the right (0-4)

Calculation    1
Formulas       2
               3
               4

Type of Column:
     0 = Calculation    1 = Text      2 = Numeric    3 = Total

Negative Numbers
   ( = Parenthesis (50.00)      – = Minus Sign  – 50.00

Press EXIT when done
```

Fig. 7-4. The Math Definition screen.

negative numbers enclosed in parentheses (rather than preceded with a minus sign).

4. If the current Math Definition settings are what you want, press F7 to get back to the Math Definition menu. If not, make your changes and then press F7.
5. Type 1 to turn Math On. The word *Math* appears at the bottom of the screen. This indicates that WordPerfect is prepared to keep track of the numbers you enter and to add them when you tell it to.
6. Enter a label for the row (if any); then press Tab to reach the first column.
7. Enter the first number in the first column (WordPerfect aligns it around the decimal point); then press Tab to reach the next column or Enter to reach the next line.
8. Repeat steps 6 and 7 for each row in the table.
9. Move the cursor to where each column subtotal belongs and type +. (The + symbol tells WordPerfect to prepare to calculate a subtotal.) Press Enter after the last +.
10. Press Alt and F7 to obtain the following menu:

1 Math Off; 2 Calculate; 3 Column On/Off; 4 Column Def: 0

and type 2 for Calculate. WordPerfect precedes each + symbol with the subtotal for the column.
11. Press Alt-F7 to get the menu back, then type 1 to select Math Off. The word *Math* disappears.

Now you can print the document. WordPerfect will print the numbers, but not the + symbols.

As a simple example of a column addition, recall the list we described under "Aligning Decimal Numbers" in Chapter 5. This list summarizes how much each club member has collected for charity; it looks like this:

Member	Collections
Brown, John	$1,504.36
Carlson, Ray	965.77
Decker, Patricia	1,668.43
Garnett, Vance	796.03
Evans, Sue	779.56
Gerard, Roy	1,056.90

Morton, Mary   800.00
Stevens, George   863.96

If you plan to produce a subtotal for the list, you would set a tab below the "t" in "Collections" (as you did before); then turn Math on and enter the names and amounts. When you reach the line where the subtotal is to appear, type **Total**, press Tab, type +, and press Enter. To produce the subtotal, obtain the menu (Alt-F7) and type **2** for Calculate. WordPerfect inserts the subtotal (8,435.01 in this case) ahead of +. Finally, get the menu back and turn Math Off.

Producing Totals and Grand Totals

In some tables, a column may include several subtotals. For example, a sales table for a retail store may have a subtotal for each department. With the Math feature, you can make WordPerfect add a column's subtotals to produce a total. To obtain a total, enter = (rather than +) where you want it to appear. WordPerfect will insert the total when you select Calculate from the menu.

Similarly, you can make WordPerfect add totals, to produce a *grand total*. Do this by entering * where the grand total belongs.

Operating on Rows

Sometimes you want to perform math operations *across* the columns of a table instead of (or as well as) *down* them. For example, if the columns in your table represent monthly sales figures for each product your company sells, you may want to add the rows to produce sales for the year. You may also want to produce an additional column showing net profits (sales minus costs). WordPerfect will perform these and other calculations if you simply set up a *Calculation column* and enter a formula that tells it what kind of calculation to make.

A calculation formula tells WordPerfect which column (or columns) to include in the calculation and how to combine them. For example, if column C is a Calculation column and you enter the formula $A + B$ into it, WordPerfect will add the numbers in column A to those in column B and display the sum in column C.

Plus (+) is just one symbol you can use in calculation formulas. WordPerfect also lets you use – (subtract), * (multiply), and / (divide). The following are typical formulas:

Formula	Tells WordPerfect to . . .
A + B – C	Add columns A and B; then subtract column C from the result.
B*.06	Multiply column B by 0.06 (to calculate sales tax, perhaps).
B/C	Find the ratio of column B to column C.
B/C*100	Find the ratio of B to C, and display it as a percentage.

You can also use parentheses in a calculation formula, to keep WordPerfect from getting confused. For example,

$(A + B)/3$

yields one-third the sum of columns A and B. If you omit the parentheses, Word-Perfect would add column A to one-third the value in column B.

There are also four special formulas you can use in Calculation columns:

+	Add numbers in the Numeric columns
+/	Average numbers in the Numeric columns
=	Add numbers in the Total columns
=/	Average numbers in the Total columns

Note that these are complete formulas; you cannot combine them with column names or numeric values.

To define a Calculation column, obtain the Math Definition screen (shown previously in Fig. 7-4); then do the following:

1. Press the right-arrow key to reach the Type number for the column; then type **0** (zero) to make it a Calculation column. WordPerfect moves to the Calculation Formulas list and displays the column letter.
2. Enter the formula for that column (note that you can define up to four Calculation columns).
3. Define the rest of the columns in the table; then press F7 to return to the menu.

Once you have set up a Calculation column, WordPerfect will insert an exclamation point (!) whenever you Tab to it. As with subtotals, totals, and grand totals, the result of the calculation will not appear until you select Calculate from the menu.

As a typical application for a Calculation column, suppose you are writing a report that is to summarize Second Quarter sales for 1986 and compare them to sales for the same period of 1985. If column A lists the 1986 figures for each sales region and column B lists 1985 figures for the same regions, you might want to make column C display the dollar difference between the two years. To do this, define A and B as Numeric columns and C as a Calculation column. The calculation formula for column C would be *A – B*.

You could also define column D as another Calculation column, and make it display the percent change between 1985 and 1986. Column D's calculation formula would be *C/B*100*.

Editing Math Tables

If you change data in a table after you perform a calculation, you must make

WordPerfect recalculate any answer the change affects. That is, make your changes (but be sure *Math* is still on the screen), and press Alt-F7 to obtain the Math menu. When it appears, select Calculate. WordPerfect replaces the original answers with the corrected ones.

You can also insert new lines or delete old ones just as you would insert or delete in a regular text table. After inserting or deleting, simply recalculate.

DRAWING LINES AND BOXES

WordPerfect also lets you draw lines and boxes in documents. This is particularly useful for creating bar charts and decorative borders. To draw a line or box, move the cursor to where you want it to begin, then press Ctrl and F3 to give a Screen command. When the following menu appears:

0 Rewrite; 1 Window; 2 Line Draw; 3 Ctrl/Alt keys;
4 Colors; 5 Auto Rewrite: 0

type **2** for Line Draw. The bottom of the screen shows

1 ¦; 2 ¦¦; 3 ∗; 4 Change; 5 Erase; 6 Move: 1

The first three options (single line, double line, and asterisk) are suggested characters you may want to use for drawing. Typing **4** for *Change* lets you substitute one of eight other characters—or any character of your choice (say, $, #, or @)—for the asterisk.

If you use Change, WordPerfect replaces the asterisk with your new character. (Of course, in any case, your printer must be able to produce the character you use for drawing. If you're not sure it can, use the character in question to draw a simple figure, then print it.)

Note that WordPerfect assumes you want to use the single line (option 1). If you want the double line, asterisk or some other character, type **2, 3** or **4**. After doing that, simply start moving the cursor using the arrow keys; WordPerfect will draw the line. If you change direction, it will insert a corner. When you finish drawing, press F1 or F7 to get back to editing.

You can also erase a drawing, or any part of it. To do this, move the cursor to where you want to start erasing, then obtain the Line Draw menu and select *Erase*. WordPerfect will then erase every character the cursor passes. To leave the Erase mode, make another choice from the menu or press F1.

The final Line Draw option, *Move*, lets you move the cursor through the drawing without affecting any of its characters. This is handy for adding lines to a drawing or positioning the cursor for an Erase.

QUESTIONS AND ANSWERS

Question. I set up a math table to keep track of sales for my business. It has three columns—receipts, sales tax, and profits—and a subtotal at the bottom for each one. However, I don't think WordPerfect added correctly. When it added sales taxes of $32.76, $27.94, and $19.32, it produced a subtotal of $80.03. Adding this on my pocket calculator, I got $80.02. What's wrong?

Answer. Probably nothing. WordPerfect calculates numbers to four digits to the right of the decimal point. But since you only asked it to display two digits, it *rounded off* the answers. To calculate the subtotal, though, it included these invisible extra digits. Figure out each sales tax value on your calculator and then add them; I'll bet $80.03 is correct!

Question. Someone submitted a report that has several columns of numbers, and I want to add each of them. Can I use the Math feature to do this?

Answer. You can, as long as the person who created the columns used Tab Align (Ctrl-F6), rather than Tab, to enter the numbers. First you must convert each table to WordPerfect's Math format. To do this, move the cursor to the beginning of the table and press Alt-F7 to select *Math/Columns*.

When the menu appears, select *Math Def*, specify the column parameters, and then turn *Math On*. WordPerfect shows *Math* at the bottom to indicate that this is a Math table. Move the cursor where you want the subtotal, type +, and press Enter. Finally, obtain the menu and select *Calculate*; then select *Math Off* to leave Math mode.

HINTS AND WARNINGS

1. If you accidentally mark the wrong text (or mark too much or too little text) for inclusion in a table of contents, list, or index, use Reveal Codes to find the [Mark:ToC,n], [Mark:List,n], or [Index:text] code at the beginning of the text, and delete it.
2. Once WordPerfect begins numbering text, it continues that numbering sequence until you tell it to restart at "1." To make it restart, use the Mark Text commands's *Define* option to select a style (the current style or a different one.)
3. In the Math feature's Math Definition screen, the *Negative Numbers* and *# of digits to the right* parameters only tell WordPerfect how to display answers;

they have nothing to do with how you enter data.

For example, you may enter negative numbers with either minus signs or parentheses, irrespective of the *Negative Numbers* setting. Similarly, you may always enter as many digits as you want after a decimal point.

4. Note that when the Math feature is on, WordPerfect always aligns numeric columns around a decimal point, even though you use Tab to move between columns. This differs from the regular editing mode, where you must press Ctrl-F6 to reach the tab position for an aligned number.

5. When recalculating answers after you have changed a math table, make sure the word *Math* appears at the bottom of the screen. If it doesn't, you won't be able to recalculate.

KEY POINT SUMMARY

Table 7-1 summarizes the keys we introduced in this chapter.

1. WordPerfect can automatically number titles in an outline or paragraphs in a document. It provides up to seven levels of numbering and three different styles: Paragraph, Outline, and Legal. To obtain automatic numbering, press Alt-F5 to give a Mark Text command.

2. To start numbering an outline, select *Outline* from the Mark Text menu; then press Enter to reach the place where the outline is to start. WordPerfect inserts the first number (I or 1) there. Press Indent or space bar to reach the place where the title is to start; then type it and press Enter.

3. To produce another first-level title, enter it as in step 2; to produce a second-level title, press Tab before you enter it.

4. To turn outlining off, do another Mark Text command and select *Outline* again.

5. You can also make WordPerfect number titles and paragraphs in a document. Move the cursor to the line where numbering is to start and (if appropriate) Tab to the number's position on the line. Then select *Para #* from the Mark Text menu. When the *Paragraph Level* prompt appears, do one of three things:

- Press Enter to produce an *automatic* number that reflects the number of previous Tabs.

Key(s)	Function
Ctrl-F3	Screen
Alt-F5	Mark Text
Alt-F7	Math/Columns

Table 7-1. Keys Introduced in Chapter 7.

- Type a digit between 1 and 7 to produce a *fixed* number at the specified level.
- Press F1 to return to editing.

6. WordPerfect uses the Outline numbering style automatically, but you can make it switch to Paragraph, Legal, or a style of your own design at any time. To switch numbering styles, select the Mark Text command's *Define* option. This option is also handy for making WordPerfect restart the numbering from "1."

7. WordPerfect will generate a table of contents if you tell it what to include. You can specify any of five different numbering styles, including no page numbers, a page number following each entry, or page numbers at the right-hand margin.

8. To register an entry in a table of contents, highlight it in Block mode, and then select *Table of Contents* from the Mark Text menu. When *ToC Level* appears, type a number between 1 and 5 to specify the indentation level of the entry.

9. After building a table of contents, you must tell WordPerfect how to display it. To do this, select *Define* from the Mark Text menu and then *Table of Contents* from the Marking Text Definition menu. Specify the number of levels (up to five) and the format (*Page Number Position*) for each level.

10. To produce a table of contents, move the cursor to where you want it to appear; then select *Generate* from the Mark Text menu.

11. Producing an index requires the same three steps as producing a table of contents. That is, you build the index by selecting entries, define the numbering style, and then generate it.

12. To add an entry to an index, move the cursor to the start of it, and if it is a phrase, highlight it in Block mode. Then select *Index* from the Mark Text menu. When the *Index Heading* prompt appears, you call tell WordPerfect that the entry is either a heading or a subheading.

13. To make an entry a heading, press Enter. When the prompt *Subheading:* appears at the bottom of the screen, enter a subheading (if you want one); then press Enter.

    To make the entry a subheading, type a heading and press Enter. When *Subheading:* and your entry appears at the bottom of the screen, press Enter.

14. After building an index, you must tell WordPerfect how to display it. To do this, select *Define* from the Mark Text menu and then *Index* from the Marking Text Definition menu. When the Index Definition menu appears, select the style you want by typing its number.

15. To produce an index, move the cursor to the end of your document and then select *Generate* from the Mark Text menu.

16. WordPerfect can also produce up to five lists that show the page locations of words and phrases in a document. This is especially convenient for producing summary lists of figures and tables.

17. Producing a list requires the same three steps as producing a table of contents or index. That is, you build the list by selecting entries, define the numbering style, and generate it.

18. To mark an entry for a list, move the cursor to the start of it and highlight it in Block mode. Then select *List* from the Mark Text menu. When the *List #* prompt appears, type the number of the list you want to produce.

19. After building a list, you must tell WordPerfect how to display it. To do this, select *Define* from the Mark Text menu and then select the appropriate list from the Marking Text Definition menu. When the List Definition menu appears, select the style you want by typing its number.

20. To produce a list, move the cursor to where you want it and select *Generate* from the Mark Text menu.

21. To update a table of contents, index, or list, repeat the procedures I have just described, but when WordPerfect asks *Have you deleted your old Table of Contents, Lists, and Index?*, press Enter or type n. This makes WordPerfect highlight the existing table, index, or list and show *Delete Block? (Y/N) N*; type y to delete it.

22. WordPerfect can perform math operations on numeric tables. It can add a column of numbers to produce a subtotal, add subtotals to produce a total, and add totals to produce a grand total. WordPerfect can also perform calculations on the rows in a table. It can add, subtract, multiply, or divide rows of numbers based on simple formulas that you enter.

23. To perform mathematical operations, set a tab for each column, press Alt-F7 to give a Math/Column command, and select *Math Def* from the menu. When the Math Definition screen appears, specify the Type for each column (Calculation, Text, Numeric, or Total) and how you want results displayed (negative numbers in parentheses or preceded by a minus sign, and the number of digits to the right of the decimal point). Press F7 when you finish.

24. When you enter data in a math table, WordPerfect aligns it around the decimal point automatically. Press Tab to move between columns.

25. To request a column subtotal, total, or grand total, type +, =, or *. WordPerfect produces these results when you select Calculate from the menu.

26. WordPerfect can perform more complex math on rows than it can on columns. Specifically, you can define up to four columns as Calculation columns, and enter a formula for each one. Math formulas may be comprised of column values, numbers, and the math symbols + (add), – (subtract), * (multiply), and / (divide).

27. To define a Calculation column, obtain the Math Definition screen and change the column's Type to *0*. When WordPerfect puts the cursor in the Column Formulas list, enter the formula.

28. Once you have set up a Calculation column, WordPerfect will insert an exclamation point whenever you Tab to it. It will calculate answers for that column when you select Calculate from the menu.

29. WordPerfect lets you draw lines in a document using a character of your

choice. To begin, move the cursor to where you want the first line to begin and press Ctrl-F3 to give a Screen command. When the Screen menu appears, select Line Draw; when the Line Draw menu appears, choose the line-drawing character from those WordPerfect has suggested (single line, double line, or asterisk), or select *Change* to specify some other character. Once you have selected a character, WordPerfect will reproduce it wherever you move the cursor. To leave the line-drawing mode, press F1.

Chapter 8

Sorting

Many people need to work with lists or tables whose entries are arranged in some specific order. A telephone list is an obvious example; it must be arranged alphabetically. A mailing list is another; companies generally want it sorted by Zip code, to take advantage of bulk postage rates. Further, an accountant may want accounts receivables listed chronologically, with the most delinquent accounts first. Regardless of what kind of list or table you have, WordPerfect can usually sort it to meet your needs.

WordPerfect can *sort* lines, paragraphs, or groups of text in a document in either ascending or descending order. Moreover, it can perform the sort on up to nine *key words*. This means, for example, that you can make it sort a telephone list by both last name (the main key word) and first name (the secondary key word), to break "ties."

Further, you can make WordPerfect sort material that is on the screen or in a file on disk. Similarly, you can tell it to display the result on the screen or store it on disk.

Finally, WordPerfect can *select* entries from a list based on criteria you specify. For example, you can request a list of customers who live in Florida, or a list of those whose accounts are delinquent, or both (all delinquent Floridians).

GENERAL PROCEDURE FOR SORTING

Before starting a sort operation, you must tell WordPerfect the following (in this general order):

- Where to obtain the sort material (from the screen or a disk file).
- Where to send the sorted result (to the screen or a disk file).
- Whether to sort by lines, paragraphs, or groups of text.
- The type of each key word (whether it is a word or number).
- The location of each key word (its position on the line and, for paragraphs and groups, its line number).
- Whether to sort in ascending or descending order.

A SIMPLE ONE-KEY SORT OPERATION

In Chapter 2, you created a telephone list (PHONE.LST) and performed some disk operations on it. That list was already in alphabetical order, because we had not yet discussed sorting. When you are creating your own computerized telephone list, however, you would probably want to enter the names and numbers in any order and then make the computer sort them. Let's consider an example.

Suppose you have entered the telephone list shown in Fig. 8-1 and saved it on disk. (**Important:** Unless you're an expert at sorting, *always save your file to disk before you sort*. That way you can start over if you foul up the sort operation.) Sort the list as follows:

1. Press Ctrl-F9 to give a Merge/Sort command.
2. When this menu appears at the bottom of the screen:

1 Merge; 2 Sort; 3 Sorting Sequences: 0

type **2** for |*Sort*|.

```
Tyner, Mavis          965-2694
Lane, Lois            557-1332
Edgewood, Bill        847-3896
Grayson, Edgar        744-6743
Grayson, Dr. Leonard  931-5410
Brown, Byron          356-7732
Carlson, Joan         753-6844
Michelle, Pam         602-5419
Raymond, Morris       705-5537
```

Fig. 8-1. A telephone list for sorting.

3. When WordPerfect shows

Input file to sort: (Screen)

press Enter.

4. Press Enter again when this prompt appears:

Output file for sort: (Screen)

WordPerfect shows the Tab Ruler, followed by its Sort menu (Fig. 8-2). The Sort menu looks fairly complex, so instead of trying to do anything with it (we will, later), let's just proceed and see what happens. After all, it does show *Sort by Line* at the top—and that's what we want to do. So, with the Sort menu on the screen, type 1 to select *Perform Action* (i.e., sort by line).

The Sort menu disappears and WordPerfect instantly sorts the list. Now the list looks like Fig. 8-3. Note that WordPerfect sorted the list correctly except

```
----------------------------------------------- Sort by Line ------------------------------------------------
Key Typ Field Word            Key Typ Field Word            Key Type Field Word
1   a    1     1              2                              3
4                             5                              6
7                             8                              9

Select

 Action                        Sort                          Type of Sort
Sort                          Ascending                     Line Sort


1 Perform Action; 2 View; 3 Keys; 4 Select; 5 Action: 6 Order;
7 Type: 0
```

Fig. 8-2. The Sort menu.

```
Brown, Byron                356-7732
Carlson, Joan               753-6844
Edgewood, Bill              847-3896
Grayson, Dr. Leonard       931-5410
Grayson, Edgar              744-6743
Lane, Lois                  557-1332
Michelle, Pam               602-5419
Raymond, Morris             705-5537
Tyner, Mavis                965-2694
```

Fig. 8-3. The telephone list after first sort operation.

for one thing: it put Dr. Leonard Grayson ahead of Edgar Grayson. Apparently, it thought "Dr." was a first name!

To put the list in proper order, you must sort by first names as well as last names. This involves telling WordPerfect where to find a first name on any given line. To do this, you must know something about how WordPerfect handles entries in a sort list—and that entails understanding the special terminology the WordPerfect manual uses for sort operations. The manual refers to *records, fields,* and *words.*

RECORDS, FIELDS, AND WORDS

A *record* is an individual entry (a line or paragraph) in the document Word-Perfect is to sort. For example, each name and number in a telephone list is a record.

A *field* is a portion of a record. For example, our sample telephone list has two fields: name and number. WordPerfect numbers fields from left to right, and requires you to separate them with indents or tabs.

A *word* is a unit that makes up a field. As expected, words are divided by spaces. WordPerfect can count words within a field from left to right (if you give it a regular number such as 1, 2, or 3) or from right to left (if you give it a negative number such as -1 or -2).

You would count words right to left if a field can contain various numbers of words. For example, our telephone list's name field contains two words (last and first name) in all but one entry: "Grayson, Dr. Leonard" has a three-word name field in which the first name is the third word. Due to this single exception, to sort the list by first names as well as last names, we must use a negative number to tell WordPerfect where to find the first name. Throughout the list, the first name is always the rightmost word, so we must use -1 to identify its location. (You would also use negative numbering to sort a list in which a field contains some names that have middle initials and others that don't.)

SORTING ON TWO KEY WORDS

Now let's sort the telephone list again, but this time sort on the first name as well as the last. Begin as before, and stop when the Sort menu appears. Let's spend a few minutes discussing the Sort menu (refer back to Fig. 8-2).

The menu's header, *Sort by Line*, indicates that WordPerfect assumes you want to sort lines rather than paragraphs. (The Select option lets you sort paragraphs.) The Sort menu provides for nine *Keys* (because WordPerfect can sort up to nine levels), and each has space for a *Typ, Field,* and *Word* parameter. As before, WordPerfect assumes that you want to sort on only one key word, so it fills in the first entry. Let's discuss the parameters.

Typ, short for Type, indicates whether the key word is alphanumeric (a) or numeric (n). Here's how they differ:

- *Alphanumeric key words* can be either words or numbers. However, alphanumeric numbers must have the same length in every record. Zip codes, telephone numbers, employee numbers, and social security numbers all meet this criteria—they are always the same length.
- *Numeric key words* can only be numbers. These may be numbers of different lengths (e.g., ages, salaries, or bowling scores) and may include dollar signs, commas, and decimal points.

Field identifies which field contains the key word. Again, fields are numbered left-to-right (*1* is the first field, *2* is the second, and so on) and are separated by tabs or indents.

Word identifies which word in the field is the key word. WordPerfect can number words from left to right (with positive numbers) or from right to left (with negative numbers).

Hence, WordPerfect's automatic choices for Key 1 indicate that it wants to base the sort operation on an alphanumeric word (*Typ* is "a") that is the first word of the first field (*Word* and *Field* are both "1"). These are the correct choices for the telephone list, because our primary sort key should refer to the last names—and that is indeed what "a 1 1" does.

Now, to make WordPerfect include first names in the sort criteria, type **3** to select *Keys*. WordPerfect puts the cursor on the "a" parameter of Key 1. Press the right-arrow key three times to reach the Key 2 parameters. WordPerfect shows "a" for *Typ*. This is what we want (because first names, like last names, are alphanumeric), so press right-arrow again. Now "1" appears for both *Field* and *Word*.

Field should indeed be "1", because first names are in the leftmost field. *Word,* however, should be "– 1", because first names appear at the end of the field. To replace the *Word* value, press right-arrow to reach it, and then Backspace to delete it. Now, type **– 1** and press F7 to leave the Key part of the menu. Finally, type **1** for Perform Action. When WordPerfect finishes sorting, the telephone list should look like the one shown in Fig. 8-4.

```
Brown, Byron          356-7732
Carlson, Joan         753-6844
Edgewood, Bill        847-3896
Grayson, Edgar        744-6743
Grayson, Dr. Leonard  931-5410
Lane, Lois            557-1332
Michelle, Pam         602-5419
Raymond, Morris       705-5537
Tyner, Mavis          965-2694
```

Fig. 8-4. The final form of telephone list.

SORTING PARAGRAPHS

WordPerfect can also sort paragraphs. This is handy for arranging catalogs, bibliographies, lists of tasks, and other kinds of descriptive lists. For sorting purposes, paragraphs may be no longer than a page and must have at least one blank line or a page break between them.

To sort paragraphs, start as you would to sort lines. That is, press Ctrl-F9 for Merge/Sort, type **2** for *Sort*, and specify the *Input file* and *Output file*. When the Sort menu appears, however, type **7** for *Type* and then **3** for *Paragraph*. Word-Perfect displays a new Sort menu that has *Sort by Paragraph* at the top. The Key fields also have an additional parameter, *Line*, and look like this:

```
Key  Typ  Line  Field  Word
 1    a    1     1      1
```

As you may have guessed, the *Line* parameter indicates which line of the paragraph contains the key word. WordPerfect lets you specify lines numbers in either top-to-bottom order (where *1* is the top line) or bottom-to-top order (where *-1* is the bottom line).

So, to sort paragraphs fill in the Key(s) and then type **1** for Perform Action.

SORTING GROUPS OF TEXT

You may also want to sort groups of line-oriented information, such as names and addresses or product specifications. To do this, you must prepare the material as a so-called *secondary merge file*. Secondary merge files are used as *address files* to produce form letters, and we'll discuss form letters in a later chapter. However, since you must know how to create a secondary merge file in order to sort groups, we should discuss what such a file contains.

Secondary Merge Files

Within a secondary merge file, each entry (e.g., an individual's name and address) is called a *record*. Records are separated by "Merge E" codes, which you produce by pressing Shift-F9. WordPerfect shows ^E on the screen and moves the cursor to the next line.

Each record is comprised of *fields*. Fields are separated by "Merge R" codes, which you produce by pressing F9. WordPerfect shows ^R and moves the cursor to the next line. Fields are numbered from top to bottom; thus, *1* is the field that starts on the first line.

Note that I just said "the field that *starts* on the first line." Fields in secondary merge files can contain as many lines as you want. For example, to create an address list of business associates, you might want to make the company name field three lines long. By reserving three lines, you can construct records that require only a company name (one line), a company and division name (two lines), or a company, division, and department name (three lines). To start a new line within a field, press Enter.

You can put any number of fields in a record, but any given field must always contain the same type of information or nothing at all. For example, suppose you are creating a secondary merge file that contains the names and addresses of both your friends and business associates. If field 2 is set aside for a company name, you would enter the name and ^R for business associates, but enter only ^R for friends.

To sort secondary merge files, start as you would to sort lines or paragraphs. That is, press Ctrl-F9 for Merge/Sort, type **2** for *Sort*, and specify the *Input file* and *Output file*. When the Sort menu appears, type **7** for *Type* and then **1** for *Merge*. WordPerfect displays a new Sort menu that has *Sort Secondary Merge File* at the top. The Key fields have the same four parameters they do for paragraphs: Typ, Line, Field, and Word.

To sort a secondary merge file, enter the Key(s), press F7, and then type **1** for Perform Action.

Merge Sort Example

Figure 8-5 shows a mailing list (albeit a rather small one) you could sort as a secondary merge file. Create it like an ordinary document, but remember to enter a ^R (F9) after each field and a ^E (Shift-F9) after each record.

Suppose we want the list sorted by Zip codes and last names. To do this, save the document on disk (name it mailing.lst), and start a sort operation as usual. When the Sort menu appears, type **7** for Type, and **1** for Merge. Now you must set up the Keys to select the Zip code as the Key 1 and the last name as Key 2.

The Zip code is a number, the second word in the fifth field (which is also

```
        Mr. Harold S. Woods^R
        Woods Flying School^R
        13 Paris Circle^R
        Ocala,^R
        FL 32787^R
        ^E
        Mr. Phillip T. Grange^R
        Newton Plastics Corporation^R
        1865 Industrial Way^R
        Newton,^R
        FL 32786^R
        ^E
        Mr. Terry Briggs^R
        Modern Designs, Inc.^R
        17565 Canard St.^R
        Newton,^R
        FL 32786^R
        ^E
        Dr. Howard L. Alberts^R
        ^R
        1305 Sunnyland Rd.^R
        Newton,^R
        FL 32786^R
        ^E
        Mrs. Viola Wilson^R
        Wilson & Associates, Inc.^R
        4399 Beach St.^R
        Ocala,^R
        FL 32787^R
        ^E
```

Fig. 8-5. A secondary merge file before sorting.

the fifth line). Type **3** to choose Keys and change Key 1 to

Key	Typ	Line	Field	Word
1	n	5	5	2

The last name is an alphanumeric word, the last word of the first field and line. (Note that I said *last* word because some records have four words in the first field, while others have three. Hence, you must enter − 1 for the Word value.) Move the cursor to the Key 2 field and enter

Key	Typ	Line	Field	Word
2	a	1	1	− 1

```
              Dr. Howard L. Alberts^R
              ^R
              1305 Sunnyland Rd.^R
              Newton,^R
              FL 32786^R
              ^E
              Mr. Terry Briggs^R
              Modern Designs, Inc.^R
              17565 Canard St.^R
              Newton,^R
              FL 32786^R
              ^E
              Mr. Phillip T. Grange^R
              Newton Plastics Corporation^R
              1865 Industrial Way^R
              Newton,^R
              FL 32786^R
              ^E
              Mrs. Viola Wilson^R
              Wilson & Associates, Inc.^R
              4399 Beach St.^R
              Ocala,^R
              FL 32787^R
              ^E
              Mr. Harold S. Woods^R
              Woods Flying School^R
              13 Paris Circle^R
              Ocala,^R
              FL 32787^R
              ^E
```

Fig. 8-6. The secondary merge file before sorting.

Finally, press F7 to leave the Keys form, and type **1** to start sorting. The sorted list should look like the one shown in Fig. 8-6.

SELECTING

WordPerfect can also select records from a list and generate a second, "result" list, based on criteria you specify. For example, if the main list contains employee information for a company, you could tell WordPerfect to produce a list of Marketing personnel or people who earn more than $30,000.

You can also combine criteria. You could, for example, request a list of Marketing and Engineering personnel who earn more than $30,000. WordPerfect normally produces the result list in sorted form, but you can request it unsorted.

Select Statements

To make WordPerfect select records from a list, you must give it the ground rules. If WordPerfect was a human being, you could simply tell it something like "List all of my customers who live in Utah." and it would do that. Being a computer program, however, WordPerfect doesn't understand plain English. But it *does* understand commands entered in the form of a so-called *select statement*.

A select statement tells WordPerfect which Key (or Keys) to use for selecting and what criteria to apply to it. For example, if Key 3 refers to state abbreviations in a customer list, the select statement

key3 = UT

tells WordPerfect to select the records for all the customers who live in Utah.

The equal sign (=) is just one symbol you can use in select statements. WordPerfect provides eight symbols in all; they are the following:

+	(OR)	combines two key definitions, and tells WordPerfect to select records that satisfy *either* condition.
*	(AND)	also combines two key definitions, but it tells WordPerfect to select records that satisfy *both* conditions.
=		Equal to
< >		Not equal to
>		Greater than
<		Less than
> =		Greater than or equal to
< =		Less than or equal to

Figure 8-7 shows a list of names and credit limits from which we could make WordPerfect select records. Some typical select statements include the following:

```
(Name)          (Init.)   (ST)   (Credit Limit)

Simpson         L         TX      75,000.
Chang           P         PA     150,000.
Albers          B         CA     300,000.
Massey          C         MD      95,000.
Wilder          G         CA     425,000.
Chamberlain     I         MD     600,000.
Raymond         S         CA      80,000.
Anderson        H         FL     160,000.
Gladstone       W         CA     150,000.
Acerson         J         UT     250,000.
```

Fig. 8-7. The credit limit list.

Statement	Selects records of . . .
key3 = UT + key3 = TX	clients from Utah or Texas
key3 = CA * key4 > 80,000	California clients whose credit limit is more than $80,000
key3 = MD * key4 = 95,000	Maryland clients whose credit limit is $95,000
key3 < > MD	all clients except those from Maryland
key4 > = 75,000	clients whose credit limit is $75,000 or more
key4 > 75,000 * key4 > 100,000	clients whose credit limit is between $75,000 and $100,000 (exclusive)

Note this about the format of select statements: You must enter a space between + or * symbols and *key* names, but enter other symbols and words (or numbers) with no space between them.

You can also use parentheses in a select statement, to keep WordPerfect from getting confused. For example,

key4 > 75,000 * (key3 = TX + key3 = PA)

selects all clients in Texas and Pennsylvania whose credit limit is more the $75,000. If you omit the parentheses, WordPerfect would select Texas clients whose credit limit is more than $75,000 and *all* Pennsylvania clients.

Finally, WordPerfect lets you use a shortcut to select all the records that contain a certain key word, regardless of which field it's in or where it's located within a field. To do this, simply type **g** after *key*. For example,

keyg = American

would select Acme American, Inc,, American Buggywhip Corp., and every other record that contains the word *American.*

Now that you know something about select statements, we can discuss how to use them to select and sort a list.

The Select and Sort Procedure

To perform a select and sort operation on a list, retrieve it from disk (or create it and save it), then do the following:

1. Start a sort operation as usual, by pressing Ctrl-F9 and choosing Sort from the menu.
2. When the Sort menu appears, use the Keys option to set up your keys. Unless you're using the "keyg" form of the select statement, be sure to enter Key parameters for the field(s) you want to select as well as those you want to sort. Press F7 when you finish.
3. Type **4** to choose *Select* from the menu. WordPerfect replaces the menu with a list of the available select statement symbols.
4. Enter your select statement, and press F7 to get back to the menu.
5. Type **1** for *Perform Action*. WordPerfect sorts and selects, and then displays the result.

Selecting Without Sorting

Sometimes you may want to select records without sorting them. For example, with a long list that's already sorted, you can save some time by just selecting from it. You may also want to skip the sorting if you plan to select from two different lists and then combine them (Retrieve one into the other) and sort the result.

To select without sorting, enter your select statement; then choose *Action* from the Sort menu. When the screen shows

1 Select and Sort; 2 Select Only: 0

type **2**.

USING SORTED MATERIAL IN A DOCUMENT

Whenever WordPerfect performs a sort operation, it sorts the *entire document*. This can produce unexpected results if you include regular text as well as the actual list. For example, if you sort a list that has a title, WordPerfect will put your title at the appropriate place in the resulting sorted list. To avoid this kind of problem, you could prepare the material to be sorted as a separate document.

An easier solution is to define the material as a block and then sort the block. To do this, obtain Block mode, highlight the material to be sorted, then continue defining the sort menu. Finally, when you tell WordPerfect to sort, it will sort only the highlighted material; the remainder of the document will be unaffected.

QUESTIONS AND ANSWERS

Question: I want to publish an alphabetized list of new members and their telephone numbers in our club's monthly newsletter. When I sorted the list, however, WordPerfect mixed other parts of the newsletter in with the list. Why?

Answer: WordPerfect sorted your entire document. To sort a portion of a document (the list, in your case), highlight it in Block mode list and then sort the block.

Question: I created a telephone list that has four fields on each line: last name, first name, area code, and telephone number. For local numbers, I omitted the area code by pressing Tab to reach the telephone number field. How can I produce a new list that contains only the entries with local numbers?

Answer: You must perform a select and sort operation in which WordPerfect selects records that have empty area code fields. To do this, save your list on disk and start a Sort operation. When the Sort menu appears, use the Type option to choose *Line*; then set up Keys for the last name, first name, and area code fields. Key 1, 2, and 3 should be "a 1 1", "a 2 1", and "n 3 1", respectively.

Next, choose the *Select* option and enter the select statement **key3 < 100** (because area codes are three-digit numbers) and press F7 to Exit. Finally, type **1** for *Perform Action*. WordPerfect will produce a list in which the area code field is empty; these are your local-number records.

HINTS AND WARNINGS

1. Sort operations don't always produce the results you expected. To keep out of trouble, save the document on disk before you sort. That way, you can always retrieve the original and start over.
2. Generally, you should make WordPerfect output sort results to the screen rather than to a disk file. This lets you determine whether the sort worked as you expected before you save it on disk.
3. Once you perform a sort operation, WordPerfect assumes you want to do the same kind of sort the next time. Always check the Sort menu's *Sort, Type of Sort,* and *Key* settings before you proceed.

4. When creating a secondary merge file, enter the Merge R code (^R) directly after each field and a ^E after each record—even the last one. If you put a space between the final character and ^R, the sort operation will not work properly.
5. If you want to sort a secondary merge file that includes a field with several lines, be careful what *Line* values you specify for key words. If a field contains more than one, count lines from the top using positive numbers, or from the bottom using negative numbers.
6. When performing a select operation, remember to enter Key parameters for every key in your select statement. To sort as well as select, you must also define Key parameters for the sorting keys.

KEY POINT SUMMARY

Table 8-1 summarizes the keys we introduced.

1. WordPerfect can sort a document by lines, paragraphs, or groups of text in either ascending or descending order, on up to nine keys. It can sort material on the screen or in a disk file, and can return the result to the screen or to disk.
2. The sort document that contains groups of text is called a *secondary merge file*.
3. Sort documents consist of records, fields, and words. Paragraphs and entries in a secondary merge file also consist of individual lines.
4. A *record* is an entry in the line, paragraph, or secondary merge file document WordPerfect is to sort. Records are separated by blank lines in a paragraph sort and by Merge E (^E) codes in a merge sort.
5. A *field* is a portion of a record. Fields are separated by Tabs or Indents in lines and paragraphs, and by Merge R (^R) codes in secondary merge files.
6. A *word* is a unit within a field; words are separated by spaces.
7. A *line* is an entire record in a line sort, a portion of a record in a paragraph sort, and all or a portion of a field in a merge sort. Lines end with Enter.
8. To start a sort operation, press Ctrl and F9 to do a Merge/Sort command; then select *Sort* from the Merge/Sort menu. When requested, tell WordPerfect where to obtain the sort document and where to send the result (screen or disk file).
9. Options in the Sort menu let you choose the *Type* of sort (Merge, Line, or

Table 8-1. Keys Introduced in Chapter 8.

Key(s)	Function
F9	Merge R (end of field in a secondary merge file)
Ctrl-F9	Sort
Shift-F9	Merge E (end of record in a secondary merge file)

Paragraph) and the *Order* (Ascending or Descending). The *Keys* option moves the cursor to the first parameter for Key 1.

10. The Key form lets you tell WordPerfect which word (or words) are to be used for sorting. There are nine Keys, for the nine possible sort levels. Key 1 has the highest priority, Key 2 has second priority, and so on.

11. For a line sort, the Key form has three parameters: Typ, Field, and Word. For paragraph and merge sorts, it has an additional parameter, Line.

12. *Typ*, short for Type, specifies whether the key word is alphanumeric (a) or numeric (n). Alphanumeric key words can be either words or numbers. Alphanumeric numbers must have the same length in every record. Numeric key words can only be numbers. These may be numbers of different lengths and may include dollar signs, commas, and decimal points.

13. *Line* specifies which line the key word is on for a paragraph or merge sort. Lines are usually counted from top to bottom in a record, but you can count them from bottom to top by using negative numbers (e.g., – 1 is the bottom line, – 2 is next-to-bottom, and so on).

14. *Field* specifies which field the key word is in. Fields can be counted left to right (or top to bottom, in a secondary merge file) by using positive numbers, or right to left by using negative numbers.

15. Use the arrow keys to move between keys and between parameters within them. Press Backspace to delete a parameter. When you finish defining keys, press F7 to return to the menu.

16. To begin a sort operation, choose *Perform Action* from the Sort menu.

17. WordPerfect lets you select records from a list, to produce a second list. To do this, you must specify the selection criteria by entering a select statement. To enter a select statement choose *Select* from the Sort menu.

18. A select statement consists of a sequence of select conditions. Each condition tells WordPerfect what criteria to apply to a specific key. For example,

key4 > = 12

tells it to select records for which Key 4 has a value of 12 or more.

19. To sort a portion of a document, highlight it in Block mode and then sort the block.

Chapter 9

Macros

Most work involves a certain amount of repetition. For example, unless you're printing correspondence on letterhead paper, you must enter your return address and date at the top each time. Further, if you regularly prepare documents such as price quotations, legal contracts, and response letters, you must usually enter some of the same paragraphs (or similar paragraphs) in each one. Besides text, your work may also require you to repeat certain WordPerfect commands. For instance, if you often include single-spaced lists or tables in a double-spaced document, you must change the spacing (and perhaps the margins and tabs) before and after the table.

With WordPerfect, you can save yourself from typing the same sequence of keystrokes every time by storing them as a *macro*. *A macro is simply a sequence of keystrokes (text character keys or command keys) that WordPerfect plays back when you tell it to.* That is, it makes WordPerfect perform like an actor reading from a script.

Of course, besides saving typing time, macros also provide some side benefits. For example, when using a macro to reproduce a block to text, you needn't worry about misspellings or typing mistakes. If you entered error-free text into the macro, WordPerfect will always replay it without errors. Moreover, because a computer is replaying the text, it will appear faster than anyone could type it. Finally, using macros to replay key commands saves you from having to remember them. Considering the many key combinations that WordPerfect furnishes for commands, you probably appreciate the benefit of that.

In addition to regular text and WordPerfect key commands, macros may include *pause* commands that let you insert information from the keyboard. The pause command is convenient for producing macros that include personalized items such as names or addresses. Typical macro users include the following:

- Attorneys who want to produce stock or *boilerplate* paragraphs that refer to a specific person or company.
- Businesspeople who want to use a form letter to reply to someone who has requested the address of a local dealer or the price of a specific item.
- Engineers who want to prepare status reports that include variable items (e.g., dates, manpower estimates, and costs) within set tables or blocks of text.
- Anyone who wants to produce periodic meeting notices or bulletins that differ only in time, place, or purpose.

Macros may also include an *Escape* feature that makes WordPerfect repeat the macro a specific number of times.

TYPES OF MACROS

WordPerfect lets you define two different kinds of macros. *Permanent macros* are those you define for use in any document; they are stored on disk, and remain there until you erase them. *Temporary macros* are those you define for use within a particular document; they are stored in memory, and disappear when you leave the document or turn the computer off.

In the course of defining a macro, WordPerfect asks what you want to name it. The name determines what you must type in order to make WordPerfect replay the macro. It also tells WordPerfect whether to make the macro permanent or temporary.

Naming Permanent Macros

To define a macro as permanent you must either give it a regular name (two to eight letters) or assign an Alt-key combination (Alt and a letter key) to it. Giving a macro a regular name lets you replay it by typing that name, while assigning a key combination lets you replay it by pressing those keys. There are advantages and drawbacks to each naming technique, as follows:

- Using a regular name makes the macro easy to remember, but you must explicitly perform a WordPerfect Macro command to start it.
- Using an Alt-key combination makes the macro easy to start (press Alt and the other key), but hard to remember.

For example, suppose you want to define a macro that makes WordPerfect switch to single-spacing. (This particular macro would contain the key sequence you would press to obtain single-spacing, Shift-F8, 4, 1, and Enter.) You could either name it *single* or assign it to a key combination such as Alt-S (where S stands for *single*).

In general, if you plan to use the macro often, assign a key combination to it; otherwise, give it a regular name.

Naming Temporary Macros

To define a macro as temporary, you can either press Enter or type a single letter (*A-Z*) when WordPerfect asks for its name. You would normally press Enter when you want only one temporary macro; in every other case, type a letter.

USING MACROS

I will now describe how to use permanent macros (which I refer to as simply "macros"). Using temporary macros requires a similar approach, but WordPerfect doesn't store them on disk.

To use a macro, you must first create or *define* it, and then tell WordPerfect where to play it back or *start* it.

Defining a Macro

To define a macro, do the following:

1. Press Ctrl and F10 to give WordPerfect a Macro Definition command. When the status line shows *Define Macro:*, you must enter a name for it.
2. To name a macro, either enter two to eight characters or hold the Alt key down and type a letter from A to Z.
3. When the blinking prompt *Macro Def* appears at the bottom of the screen, enter the keystrokes you want WordPerfect to play back. As we mentioned earlier, besides text, this can include tab or margin commands, special print formats (e.g., centering, bold type, underlining, superscripts, subscripts), or anything else you can use in a regular document.
4. Wherever you want WordPerfect to pause for a keyboard insertion, press Ctrl and PgUp. When the computer beeps, press Enter *twice* to continue defining the macro.
5. When you finish, press Ctrl and F10 again. WordPerfect saves the macro on your data disk and then returns to editing.
6. Erase the macro text by doing an Exit operation.

Replaying a Macro

When you reach the place in a document where you want to replay a macro, do one of two things:

- If you gave the macro a regular two- to eight-letter name, press Alt and F10. When WordPerfect shows *Macro:*, type the macro's name and press Enter.

- If you assigned the macro to an Alt-key combination, hold Alt down and press the letter key.

An Example of a Standard Reply Letter

Suppose you want to notify a customer that your company is cancelling credit due to unpaid bills. Fig. 9-1 shows the general form of a letter you could use. The line **Shift-F5 3** below the return address shows the keystrokes you must enter to make WordPerfect insert the current date. The underlined material in square brackets indicates places where WordPerfect should allow you to insert personalized items.

To define this letter as a macro, do the following:

1. Start a new document. When the blank first page appears, delete the automatic tabs and set a new tab at the center (column 42).
2. Press Ctrl-F10 to start defining a macro.
3. When WordPerfect shows the prompt *Define Macro:*, enter **nocredit**.
4. Enter the return address shown in Fig. 9-1. On the line below it, press Tab to reach the center, and then press Shift-F5 for Date. When the Date menu

```
                              211 Washington Street
                              San Diego, CA 92121
                              Shift-F5 3

[Customer's name and address]

Dear [Name]:

As of the close of business on [Date], your company has
outstanding invoices over 30 days old totaling [Amount].  We must
request immediate payment of these invoices or we will be forced
to add a 1 1/2% monthly service charge.

Until we receive payment, we cannot extend credit to your company
or process further orders.  Please remit this payment to my
attention as soon as possible.

                              Sincerely yours,




                              Marie F. Gerard
                              Assistant Credit Manager
```

Fig. 9-1. The generalized letter showing insertion points.

appears, type **3** for *Insert Function* and press Enter twice to reach the line where the customer's address belongs.

5. Press Ctrl-PgUp to insert a pause command for the customer's name. When the computer beeps, press Enter twice to continue; then press Enter once more to reach the company name line.
6. Enter pause commands for the company's name, street address, and city; then move the cursor to the salutation line.
7. Enter the start of the salutation (**Dear**) and insert a pause command for the name.
8. Complete the letter, inserting two more pause commands in the first sentence—one after "close of business on " and the other at the end of the sentence.
9. Press Ctrl-F10 to save the macro on disk.
10. Erase the macro text by doing an Exit operation.

Let's use the *nocredit* macro to produce a credit cancellation letter to Harold "Bug" Rogers of Pest-B-Gone, Inc. As of October 11, 1986, Pest-B-Gone has accumulated $1287.67 in unpaid invoices. With the screen now blank, proceed as follows:

1. Press Alt-F10 to start a macro.
2. When WordPerfect shows the *Macro:* prompt at the bottom of the screen, enter **nocredit**. WordPerfect produces the return address and date and then beeps the computer.
3. Respond to the beep by entering **Mr. Harold "Bug" Rogers**.
4. Respond to the next three beeps by entering these lines:

Pest-B-Gone, Inc.
2786 Mayflower St.
San Diego, CA 92121

5. When the computer beeps after "Dear " in the salutation, enter **Mr. Rogers**.
6. When it beeps after "close of business on ," enter **October 11, 1986**.
7. When it beeps after "totaling ," enter **$1286.67**.

When WordPerfect finishes, print the letter.

MACROS THAT REPLACE ABBREVIATIONS

In Chapter 6, I described the use of the Replace operation to expand abbreviations. Using Replace, however, forces you to enter the search and replace strings each time; WordPerfect doesn't remember them from one document to the next or (in the case of the replace string) even from one Replace operation to the next. If you use an abbreviation often (say, DoD for Department of Defense or pfp for "party of the first part"), you should define a macro for it. The macro should perform a Replace command, and enter your abbreviation for the -> *Srch:* string and its expanded text for the *Replace with:* string.

For example, suppose you want to set up a macro that replaces every occurrence of *aic* in your document with "Acme International Corporation." To define it, do the following:

1. Press Ctrl-F10 to give a Macro Definition command.
2. When *Define Macro:* appears, type **aic** and press Enter.
3. When *Macro Def* appears, press Home *twice*, up-arrow, Alt-F2, and (when the *Confirm?* prompt appears) Enter.
4. When -> *Srch:* appears, press the space bar, then type aic and press F2.
5. When *Replace with:* appears, press the space bar, then type **Acme International Corporation** and press F2.
6. Press Ctrl-F10 to save the macro on disk.

After that, you can replay the *aic* macro at any time. To begin, press Alt-F10. When WordPerfect shows *Macro:*, type aic and press Enter. WordPerfect expands the abbreviations throughout the document.

MACROS THAT PERFORM COMMANDS

If you use certain commands often, you should consider defining them as macros. Not only do macros perform commands faster than you could from the keyboard, but they also let you do commands without breaking your train of thought.

To get some ideas about what macros you might develop, consider the following list. Here, each macro is assigned an appropriate Alt-key combination, but you could just as easily give them regular names. We have also listed the contents of each macro (the key sequence that defines it).

Alt-T—Change the tabs.
    Sequence: Shift-F8 1 Ctrl-End (Define tabs) F7
    Operation: Do a Line Format command to set up new tabs (Shift-F8 1) by clearing the existing ones (Ctrl-End) and defining new ones.

Alt-M— Change the margins.
    Possible use: To indent a paragraph on both sides.
    Sequence: Shift-F8 3 (Specify margins)
    Operation: Do a Line Format command to set the margins.

Alt-L—Change the line spacing.
    Sequence: Shift-F8 4 (Specify spacing)
    Operation: Do a Line Format command to set the line spacing.

Alt-D—Insert date.
> *Sequence:*   Shift-F5 1
> *Operation:*   Do a Date command (Shift-F5) and choose the Insert Text option (1).

Alt-K—Insert conditional end of page.
> *Sequence:*   Alt-F8 9 (Number of lines)
> *Operation:*   Do a Page Format command (Alt-F8), choose the Conditional End of Page option (9), and specify the number of lines to keep on this page.

Alt-S—Save document, but stay in WordPerfect.
> *Sequence:*   F10 Enter y
> *Operation:*   Save the document (F10) under the same name (Enter) and replace it on disk (y).
> *Comment:*   Only works for existing documents, not new ones.

Alt-E—Save document and clear the screen.
> *Sequence:*   F7 Enter Enter y n
> *Operation:*   Exit from the document (F7), but save it (Enter) under the same name (Enter) and replace it on disk (y). Then clear the screen or the window (n).
> *Comment:*   Only works for existing documents, not new ones.

Alt-C—Stop the print operation and cancel all print jobs.
> *Sequence:*   Shift-F7 4 c * y
> *Operation:*   Do a Print command (Shift-F7) and choose the Printer Control option (4). When the Printer Control menu appears, choose Cancel Print Jobs (c) and specify all jobs (* y).

Alt-G—Send a Go command to the printer to print the next single-sheet page.
> *Sequence:*   Shift-F7 4 g Enter
> *Operation:*   Do a Print command (Shift-F7) and choose the Printer Control option (4). When the Printer Control menu appears, choose "Go" (g) and return to editing (Enter).

REPEATING A MACRO

Sometimes you want to insert the same material several times in succession. This is particularly common when someone must prepare a list of names and addresses, product descriptions, or anything else in which the entries are similar. To create such lists from the keyboard, the operator would have to perform the entry procedure repeatedly until he or she has completed the list.

One way to eliminate some of this repetition is to define the general structure of an entry as a macro and then run that macro each time an entry is to be inserted. For example, if the list consists of names and addresses, the macro could produce the labels *Name:*, *Street Address:*, *City:*, *State:*, and *Zip Code:*, and pause after each one to let the operator fill in the information.

If, however, you know how many times you want to repeat this procedure (e.g., how many names and addresses you want to enter), you can tell WordPerfect to repeat the macro. To make it do this, press the Esc (Escape) key before you start the macro. WordPerfect shows *n = 8* at the bottom of the screen; it assumes you want to repeat the macro eight times. If that's what you want, start the macro as usual—note: *don't* press Enter before you start the macro. Otherwise, type another number e.g., type **5** to repeat the macro five times, and then start the macro.

For example, to repeat a macro called *names* 10 times, press Esc, type **10**, and press Alt-F10. When the *Macro:* prompt appears, enter **names**.

CHAINING MACROS

WordPerfect lets you call, or *start*, one macro from within another. The manual refers to this technique as *chaining* macros. The advantage of chaining is that it lets you combine a number of small macros to build bigger macros. This is like having an assortment of spices that you can choose from to make different recipes.

To chain an existing macro to a new one, define the new macro as usual, but when you get to the place where WordPerfect is to run the existing macro, enter a start command for it. WordPerfect will not actually start the second macro at this point; it will start the existing macro when you run the new one.

An Example of Format-Changing Macro

Under "Macros That Perform Commands," I described macros that change the tabs, margins, and line spacing (Alt-T, Alt-M, and Alt-L, respectively). Using chaining, you could define a fourth macro that changes all three parameters. The definition of this macro (call it Alt-F, for "Format") would be simply

Alt-T Alt-M Alt-L

Macros like this one are convenient if you regularly use different formats for various projects. (For example, you may use one format for letters, another for reports, and a third for memoranda). WordPerfect starts every new document with its built-in, or *default*, format settings. By creating format-changing macros such as Alt-F, you can switch formats by simply pressing the appropriate keys. This lets you get right to work without spending time doing format commands.

REPEATING CHAINS

If a macro includes a Search command, you can make WordPerfect repeat it until the search fails. To do this, simply chain the macro to itself, by entering the macro's name in its own definition. This feature is handy for performing replace operations without using the Replace command. For example, in Chapter 6 we mention that Replace cannot replace an uppercase phrase with a lowercase phrase, and you are better off making the replacement by doing a series of Search-delete-enter operations. Instead of manually starting each of these operations, you can define them in a macro and then make the macro call itself to repeat the operations throughout the entire document. To make a macro call itself, press Alt-F10 and enter the name you used to respond to the *Define Macro:* prompt.

For example, as I mention in Chapter 6, the Replace command will not replace "I" with "we"; because "I" is capitalized, WordPerfect will always replace it with the capitalized form "We." To make this replacement, you can define a temporary macro (call it *i*) to execute the following procedure:

1. Do a Search operation.
2. When -> *Srch:* appears, type I and press the space bar.
3. Start the search.
4. Delete the *I.*
5. Type *we* to make the replacement.
6. Call this macro, to repeat the procedure.

To define this macro, press the following keys:

F2 I space F2 Backspace we Alt-F10 i

Of course, if your document contains any Is at the beginning of sentences, WordPerfect will also replace them with the lowercase we. To correct those occurrences, do a selective Replace operation with "we" as the search string and "We" as the replacement string.

You can create similar macros to replace capitalized words. Simply use Ctrl-Backspace (rather than Backspace) in your definition. Ctrl-Backspace deletes the preceding word.

OPERATING ON MACRO FILES

Sometimes you want to operate on macro files. For example, if a macro name is inappropriate or hard to remember, you will want to rename it. Similarly, if there is a macro on your disk that you never use, you will want to delete it.

You can rename, delete, view, or copy macro files just as if they were regular document files by giving a List Files command (F5). Since you want to list only macro files, however, type b: \ *.mac (for floppy disks) or c: \ wp \ *.mac (for a hard disk) when the *Dir* prompt appears. WordPerfect always gives macro files the extension .MAC. Thus, macros with regular (two- to eight-letter) names have filenames of the form *macroname* .MAC, while Alt-key macro files have names of the form ALT*L* .MAC, where *L* is the letter.

RUNNING A MACRO AT STARTUP

In Chapter 2 (under "Editing a Disk Document"), I mentioned that Word-Perfect will load a document file when you start if you give it a command of the form **a:wp** *filename*. You can also make it run a macro at startup. To do this, enter a command of the form **a:wp/m-*macroname***. For example, if you created the format-changing macro Alt-F that we described earlier, you could start a new document with those alternate settings by entering **a:wp/m-altf**.

QUESTIONS AND ANSWERS

Question: I enter my address and the date at the top of every letter. Can I make WordPerfect enter them for me?

Answer: Yes, store the information as a macro, using the Macro Definition command (Ctrl-F10). You might name this macro *addr*. When *Macro Def* appears, type the address as you would normally. When you reach where the date should appear, press Shift-F5 to do a Date command and type **3** to insert a date code; then press Ctrl-F10 to end the macro. After that, you can press Alt-F10 and enter **addr** at the beginning of every new letter. WordPerfect will produce your address and the current date.

Question: Sometimes I forget the names of my macros. How can I get a list of them?

Answer: Press F5 to do a List Files command. When the *Dir* prompt appears, enter **b:\ *.mac** for a floppy disk or **c:\ wp \ *.mac** for a hard disk.

Question: I defined a macro that inserts a standard paragraph in contracts that I prepare. When I ran it, however, I noticed that a word is misspelled. How can I correct it?

Answer: You can correct it, if you have the macro editor included with the optional WordPerfect Library. Otherwise, you must redefine the entire macro from scratch.

Question: I wanted to repeat a macro six times, so before starting it, I pressed Esc and entered **6** for the *n* = prompt. However, WordPerfect only ran the macro once. Why?

Answer: You probably pressed Enter after typing the *6*. Try again, but this time start the macro (with Alt-F10 or Alt-key) immediately after you type the number.

HINTS AND WARNINGS

1. When defining a macro, remember to press Ctrl-F10 at the end of it as well as at the beginning. If you don't press Ctrl-F10 the second time, WordPer-

fect will simply continue building the macro indefinitely, and put everything you type into it.

2. Once you begin defining a macro, there is no way to cancel the operation. If you spot a mistake in an earlier part of the macro or want to stop for any other reason, press Ctrl-F10 to end the macro, then redefine it from scratch. When you finish, WordPerfect will replace the old version with the new one.

3. To stop a macro while it's running, press the F1 (Cancel) key.

4. WordPerfect does not itself provide a way to edit macro files. To change one, you must redefine it. If you regularly change macros, you can purchase the WordPerfect Library, which includes a macro editor.

5. A macro can contain such material as you want to put into it. Its size is limited only by the amount of storage space on your disk.

KEY POINT SUMMARY

Table 9-1 summarizes the keys we introduced.

1. A macro is a sequence of keystrokes (text or commands) that WordPerfect plays back when you tell it to.

2. There are two different kinds of macros. Permanent macros are those you define for use in any document; they are stored on disk, and remain there until you erase them. Temporary macros are those you define for use within a particular document; they are stored in memory and disappear when you leave the document or turn the power off.

3. To use a macro, you must first create, or define, it; then tell WordPerfect where to play it back, or start, it.

4. To define a macro, press Ctrl-F10 to give a Macro Definition command. When the status line shows *Define Macro:*, you must enter a name.

5. To set up a permanent macro, enter a name that has between two and eight letters, or press Alt and a letter key (A-Z). To set up a temporary macro, enter a one-letter name or press Enter.

6. When the blinking prompt *Macro Def* appears at the bottom of the screen, enter the keystrokes you want WordPerfect to play back.

7. Wherever you want WordPerfect to pause for a keyboard insertion, press

Table 9-1. Keys Introduced in Chapter 9.

Key(s)	Function
Alt-F10	Start a named macro
Alt-key	Start an Alt-key macro
Ctrl-F10	Define (create) a macro
Ctrl-PgUp	Pause command (within a macro definition)
Esc	Repeat a macro

Ctrl and PgUp. When the computer beeps, press Enter twice to continue defining the macro.

8. When you finish defining a macro, press Ctrl and F10 again.

9. To replay, or start, a macro, move the cursor to where you want it to appear and either press Alt and a letter key (if you assigned an Alt-key combination to it) or press Alt-10 and enter the name.

10. To make WordPerfect repeat a macro, press Esc. When the n = prompt appears, type the repetition count and then start the macro.

11. WordPerfect lets you chain macros that is, you can start a macro from within another macro. To include a macro in another macro's definition, insert a start command for the existing macro.

12. If a macro contains a Search operation, you can repeat the macro indefinitely by chaining it to itself. The macro will end when the search fails. To chain a macro to itself, start within its own definition.

13. You can rename, delete, view, or copy macro files just as if they were regular document files, by giving a List Files command (F5). Since you want to list only macro files, however, type **b:\ *.mac** (for floppy disks) or **c:\ wp \ .mac** (for a hard disk) when the *Dir* prompt appears.

14. To make WordPerfect run a macro at startup, enter a command of the form **a:wp/m-*macroname*.**

Chapter 10

Form Letters

Sometimes you must send the same letter (such as a request for payment, notice of credit terms, order acknowledgment, or report on account status) to an entire list of recipients. Direct mail solicitors often use personalized letters that have the recipient's name and address in various places. The following is typical of the kind of letters that fill our mailboxes and wastebaskets:

Dear Mr. Brown:

Would you like the name James C. Brown to be associated with success? Yes, Mr. Brown, you can be a dynamic, successful person if you attend our seminar.

With WordPerfect, creating this kind of personalized form letter takes three steps:

1. Prepare a model of the letter in which you name places or fields that will vary (e.g., the recipient's name, address, account number, outstanding balance, etc.)
2. Prepare a data file containing the items WordPerfect must insert into the multiple copies.
3. Use a *Merge* command to combine the form with the data and print the letters.

The WordPerfect manual refers to the generalized letter as the *primary file* and to the data file as a *secondary merge file*.

We will first discuss the simple situation in which WordPerfect replaces fields in the primary file with items from the secondary merge file on a one-for-one basis. We will then describe WordPerfect's features for creating more elaborate form letters. These include customizing letters from the keyboard and the use of macros to automate merge operations.

SIMPLE FORM LETTERS

As an example of a simple form letter, let us produce an invitation to a company's anniversary party. All we will do here is insert an individual address, a salutation, and a single reference to the recipient's affiliation. We will explain the procedures for creating a secondary merge file, entering the primary file, merging the files, and printing the copies.

Contents of a Secondary Merge File

A secondary merge file is a document containing the entries to be merged into the primary document to produce the copies. We already encountered secondary merge files in the "Sorting Groups of Text" section in Chapter 8. There, we used secondary merge files to hold entries for sorting.

As you may recall, within a secondary merge file, each entry (e.g., an individual's name and address) is called a *record*. Records are separated by Merge E codes, which you produce by pressing Shift-F9. WordPerfect shows ^E on the screen and moves the cursor to the next line.

Each record is comprised of *fields*. Fields are separated by Merge R codes, which you produce by pressing F9. WordPerfect shows ^R and moves the cursor to the next line. Fields are numbered from top to bottom; thus, *1* is the field that starts on the first line.

Fields in secondary merge files can contain as many lines as you want. For example, to create an address list of business associates, you may want to reserved three lines for the company name field. By reserving three lines, you can construct records that require only a company name (one line), a company and division name (two lines), or a company, division, and department name (three lines). To start a new line within a field, press Enter.

You can put any number of fields in a record, but any given field must always contain the same type of information or nothing at all. For example, suppose you are creating a secondary merge file that contains the names and addresses of both your friends and business associates. If field 2 is set aside for a company name, you would enter the name and ^R for business associates, but enter only ^R for friends.

Figure 10-1 shows the secondary merge file for the invitation. Each entry consists of five fields: name, company, street, city, and first name. Prepare this file just as you would any document, then save it under the name *guests.sf* where *sf* stands for secondary file. Use the Exit (F7) command to perform the save, so that you obtain a blank screen on which to enter the primary file.

```
            Mr. Phillip T. Grange^R
            Newton Plastics Corporation^R
            1865 Industrial Way^R
            Newton, FL 32786^R
            Phil^R
            ^E
            Mrs. Viola Wilson^R
            Wilson and Associates, Inc.^R
            4399 Beach St.^R
            Ocala, FL 32787^R
            Vi^R
            ^E
```

Fig. 10-1. The secondary merge file for a simple form letter.

Creating a Primary File

Now you may enter the generalized letter as shown in Fig. 10-2. As usual, use Line Format to set a tab at the center for the return address, the closing, and the writer's name and title.

The symbols ^F1^ through ^F5^ tell WordPerfect which data field to insert when printing letters. They are numbered according to the order in which fields appear in the secondary merge file; ^F1^ specifies the name field, ^F2^ specifies the company, and so on. To produce them, do the following:

1. Press Alt-F9 to give a *Merge Codes* command. WordPerfect shows the following list:

```
^C; ^D; ^F; ^G; ^N; ^O; ^P; ^Q; ^S; ^T; ^U; ^V:
```

2. Type f to select ^F. WordPerfect shows *Field Number?* at the bottom.
3. Type the number of the field you want to insert (e.g., type 1 for the name field or 2 for the company field); then press Enter. WordPerfect inserts a symbol of the form ^F*n*, where *n* is the field number.

When you finish entering the letter, save it under the name *invite.pf* (where *pf*

```
                          Gutenberg Printing, Inc.
                          1243 Flamingo Lane
                          Newton, FL 32786
                          September 24, 1986


^F1^
^F2^
^F3^
^F4^

Dear ^F5^:

This year is Gutenberg Printing's fifth anniversary in business.
To mark the occasion, we are hosting a cocktail party on
Wednesday, October 1, from 4:30 to 7:00 PM at the Newton Inn.  As
one of our most valued customers and friends at ^F2^, we would be
honored by your presence.  I hope to see you there!

                          Best wishes,



                          James A. Anderson
                          President
```

Fig. 10-2. A simple form letter before merging.

stands for primary file). As with the secondary file, use the Exit (F7) to perform the save, so you end up with a blank screen.

Merging Form Letters

To produce our personalized invitations (that is, to *merge* the primary and secondary files), proceed as follows:

1. Press Ctrl-F9 to give a *Merge/Sort* command.
2. When the following menu appears:

1 Merge; 2 Sort; 3 Sorting Sequences: 0

> type **1** to select Merge.
> 3. Enter **invite.pf** for *Primary file:* and **guests.sf** for *Secondary file:*.

WordPerfect shows **Merging** while it does the merge. When it finishes, the completed invitations appear, one per page, and the cursor is at the end of the last page.

Figure 10-3 shows the completed letter to Phillip Grange. Note that WordPerfect has replaced all the ^Fn^ symbols with specific fields from the secondary file.

Printing Form Letters

Since WordPerfect has produced the form letters as a regular document, press F7 to do a Print command and type **1** to select *Full Text*. Of course, you can also save the letters on disk as, say, *invite.ltr*.

Merging to the Printer

Sometimes you may want WordPerfect to send completed form letters to the printer instead of the screen. To make it do this, use the Merge Codes command

```
                              Gutenberg Printing, Inc.
                              1243 Flamingo Lane
                              Newton, FL 32786
                              September 24, 1986

Mr. Phillip T. Grange
Newton Plastics Corporation
1865 Industrial Way
Newton, FL 32786

Dear Phil:

This year is Gutenberg Printing's fifth anniversary in business.
To mark the occasion, we are hosting a cocktail party on
Wednesday, October 1, from 4:30 to 7:00 PM at the Newton Inn.  As
one of our most valued customers and friends at Newton Plastics
Corporation, we would be honored by your presence.  I hope to see
you there!


                              Best wishes,



                              James A. Anderson
                              President
```

Fig. 10-3. The form letter after merging.

```
┌──────────────────────────────────────────────────────────────┐
│                                                                │
│                                                                │
│   Susan Briggs                                                 │
│   Universal Bridge Co.                                         │
│   12366 West 10th Street                                       │
│   Bridge City, PA 16589                                        │
│                                                                │
│                                                                │
│                                                                │
│                                                                │
│                                                  ^F1^          │
│                                                  ^F2^          │
│                                                  ^F3^          │
│                                                  ^F4^          │
│                                                                │
│                                                                │
└──────────────────────────────────────────────────────────────┘
```

Fig. 10-4. The primary file for printing envelopes.

(Alt-F9) to put a ^T code at the end of your primary file. The ^T tells WordPerfect to send merged text up to that point. You should know, however, that merging to the printer is not only very slow, but ties up your computer; you can't do other work until merging has finished.

To print multiple copies of the form letters, do a Print command before you do the merge. When the Print menu appears, choose Printer Control (4); when the Printer Control menu appears, choose Select Print Options (1), then change Number of Copies to what you want.

Canceling a Merge Operation

Suppose that while WordPerfect is doing a merge operation, you spot a mistake in the form letter, or you suddenly realize you're merging with the wrong secondary file. When that happens, you will want to cancel the merge operation immediately. To cancel a merge, press the F1 (Cancel) key. This makes *Merging* disappear from the bottom of the screen and puts WordPerfect back in regular editing mode.

PRINTING ENVELOPES

You can also use WordPerfect to address envelopes. Here, the primary file would contain only your return address (unless you have preprinted envelopes) and ^Fn^ symbols for the recipient's name, company, street address, and city. Figure 10-4 shows a typical primary file for use on standard 4 1/8-inch by 9 1/2-inch business-size envelopes.

We have started the recipient's fields at line 12 and column 45, so they print

2 inches from the top and 4 1/2 inches from the left edge. (You may want different values.) Furthermore, printing envelopes also requires you to use your printer in hand-fed mode, so that it pauses between envelopes.

Customizing Form Letters from the Keyboard

WordPerfect lets you add information to a form letter from the keyboard. You can use this feature to insert specific dates, times, places, subjects, event names, sponsors, numbers, or messages to a generalized letter.

WordPerfect provides this capability through the merge code ^C. The ^C code makes stop and wait for you to enter text (type the text and then press F9. WordPerfect can also display a prompt on the status line when it needs keyboard information. To make it do this, precede ^C with the sequence ^O*message*^O.

For example, say you want to notify all sales representatives of their last quarter's total and current quarter's goal for a particular item. Figure 10-5 shows the standard letter. Note that we use ^F1^, ^F2^ and ^F3^ for the representative's name, street address, and city, and ^O*prompt*^O^C for last quarter's sales and this quarter's goals. Note also the ^T^N^P^P at the end, to send the copies directly to the printer.

When you merge this memorandum, WordPerfect obtains the first name and address from the secondary file and displays the memorandum. It puts the cursor at the end of the first sentence (where you entered ^OSales^O^C) and shows the prompt *Sales* at the bottom of the screen. Type the sales amount for the first representative and press F9. Type the goal amount and press F9 again when the prompt *Goal* appears. WordPerfect will now print the first memorandum and then

```
From: Richard Gordon, National Sales Manager

To: ^F1^
    ^F2^
    ^F3^

Subject: Sales for third quarter 1986.

    According to our records, your sales for the third quarter of
1986 were ^OSales^O^C.  Your goal for the current quarter is
^OGoal^O^C.  If either of these do not concur with your records,
please notify me.  These numbers will be used to calculate
commissions and determine progress toward overall sales goals.
Please acknowledge receipt of this notification and report ant
discrepancies before the end of the current quarter.
^T^N^P^P
```

Fig. 10-5. A sales memorandum using keyboard insertions.

display the second one. It repeats this procedure for each record in the secondary file.

USING MACROS WITH MERGE OPERATIONS

You can also use macros to automate merge operations. One way is to set up a macro that starts the merge and supplies the name of the primary file and perhaps the secondary file.

For example, suppose you have a form letter in a primary file called *FORM* (there is no secondary file, you insert specifics from the keyboard). To save yourself the bother of doing a Merge command each time, you could assign a merge-starting macro to the Alt-F key combination. To define the *ALTF* macro, you would do the following:

1. Press Ctrl-F9 to do a Merge/Sort.
2. Type 1 to select Merge.
3. When *Primary file:* appears, enter **form**.
4. When *Secondary file:* appears, press Enter (because there is no secondary file). WordPerfect begins merging.
5. Press Shift-F9 to end the merge and save the macro.

You can also make WordPerfect start a macro when it finishes merging. This is handy for beginning a second merge operation or for sending the merged text to the printer. To make WordPerfect proceed from merging to a macro, enter a command of the form ^G*macro name*^G at the end of your primary file.

USING MULTIPLE PRIMARY FILES

The merge code sequence ^P*filename*^P makes WordPerfect retrieve a file from the disk and use it as a new primary file. This is especially useful for building form letters from files that contain various kinds of boilerplate text. It also has the advantage that by changing only one file, you automatically change all the merge files that use it.

The similar sequence ^P^C^P lets the user enter the name of the file to be retrieved during the merge operation. The WordPerfect manual gives an example that uses these commands to "assemble" a contract.

QUESTIONS AND ANSWERS

Question: My form letter contains ^C codes to let me insert personalized data from the keyboard. However, when I merged the letter, WordPerfect stopped and let me make the first insertion, but never continued on after that. Pressing Enter simply made it move the cursor down the screen. What did I do wrong?

Answer: You pressed Enter, instead of F9, to end the insertion. Pressing F9 in regular editing mode performs a Merge R command; pressing it during a merge operation tells WordPerfect to resume merging after a keyboard insertion.

Question: WordPerfect omitted a data item from one of my form letters. Why?

Answer: You entered an empty field for that item in the addressee's record of your secondary file. That is, you entered only ^R; you should have entered the data and then ^R.

Question: I have a secondary file with the names and addresses of my company's 120-person sales staff, and I want to send a memorandum to the six Regional Managers. What's the easiest way to do this?

Answer: Create another secondary file that contains only the records for the Regional Managers and merge it with the memorandum. The easiest way to create the second file is to retrieve the original file and copy each Regional Manager's record into a new document in the second window (see "Windows" in Chapter 6). When you finish copying, save the second window on disk and then do the merge.

An alternate approach is to merge the original secondary file with the memorandum and then print only the Regional Managers' copies. Realize, however, that with a 120-record file, the merge operation may take a while.

HINTS AND WARNINGS

1. If a form letter contains only regular text and insertions from the keyboard, you need not specify a secondary merge file. When the *Secondary file:* prompt appears, press Enter.
2. Like a regular document print operation, a merge to printer operation uses the Select Print Options to determine how many copies to print. Remember that the default value is one copy printed.
3. Note that the Shift-F9 key combination has two different uses. Pressing it during editing gives WordPerfect a Merge E command, which inserts ^E (the end-of-record code) on the screen and moves the cursor to the next line. Pressing Shift-F9 during a merge operation cancels the merge.
4. The F9 key also has two uses. Pressing it during editing gives WordPerfect a Merge R command, which inserts ^R (the end-of-field code) and moves the cursor to the next line. You can also press F9 during a merge operation, to make WordPerfect resume after you have inserted text from the keyboard.

KEY POINT SUMMARY

Table 10-1 summarizes the keys and merge codes we introduced.

1. WordPerfect can produce form letters by combining a generalized letter (the *primary file*) with entries or *records* from a secondary file.
2. Within a secondary file, fields must be separated with Merge R (^R) codes, and records must be separated with Merge E (^E) codes. Produce these codes by pressing F9 and Shift-F9, respectively.
3. The primary file is a regular document that includes a field symbol of the

Table 10-1. Keys and Merge Codes Introduced in Chapter 10.

Key(s)	Function
F9	|*Within a secondary file:*| Merge R
	|*During a merge operation:*| Continue after inserting text from the keyboard
Alt-F9	Merge Codes (other than Merge E and Merge R)
Shift-F9	|*Within a secondary file:*| Merge E
	|*During a merge operation:*| Cancel the merge

Merge Code	Function
^C	Stop merging and wait for an insertion from the keyboard. When WordPerfect stops, type the text, then press F9 to resume merging.
^Fn^	Insert field |*n*| from the secondary file.
^G|*macro name*|^G	Start the named macro at the end of the merge.
^N	Look for the next record in the secondary file.
^O|*messge*| ^O^C	Display the message on the status line.
^P|*filename*|^P	Use the specified file as the new primary file.
^P^C^P	Let the user specify the new primary file.
^T	Send merged text to the printer.

form ^Fn^ wherever WordPerfect is to insert a data item. Here, ^F1^ specifies the first field in a record, ^F2^ specifies the second field, and so on.

To insert a field symbol, press Alt-F9 to obtain the Merge Codes menu and type f to select ^F. WordPerfect will prompt for the field number.

4. To produce form letters, merge a primary file with a secondary file. To do this, press Ctrl-F9 to do a Merge/Sort command and type 1 to select Merge from the menu. Enter the names of the primary and secondary files when WordPerfect asks for them.

5. WordPerfect sends completed form letters to the screen; to make it print them automatically, insert the merge code sequence ^T^N^P^P at the end of your primary file. (Again, produce these codes using the Merge Codes command.)

6. You can cancel a merge operation at any time by pressing Shift-F9 (Merge E).

7. WordPerfect lets you add information to a form letter from the keyboard. To make it do this, insert the merge code ^C where you want it to stop and let you enter text (type the text and press F9).

WordPerfect can also display a prompt on the status line when it needs keyboard information. To make it do this, precede ^C with the sequence ^O*message*^O.

8. To make WordPerfect start a macro when it finishes merging, insert the sequence ^G*macro name*^G at the end of your primary file.

9. The merge code sequence ^P*filename*^P makes WordPerfect retrieve a file from the disk and use it as a new primary file. This is useful for building form letters from files that contain various kinds of boilerplate text. The similar sequence ^P^C^P lets the user enter the name of the file to be retrieved during the merge operation.

Chapter 11

Customizing WordPerfect

When you begin working on a document, WordPerfect gives you built-in, or *default,* values for its various system parameters. For example, if you use Word-Perfect in its original form, it sets the left-hand margin at column 10 and the right-hand margin at column 74, and puts tabs at every fifth column (5, 10, 15, and so on). It also assumes that you want to print 54 single-spaced lines on 11-inch paper, right-justified, starting one inch from the top of every page and one inch from the left-hand edge.

These are WordPerfect's guesses at what you need for most work. If they are not right for you, you can select more convenient ones. For example,

- If you want shorter lines or double space most material, you can alter the line format to produce these features automatically.
- If you print on legal-size or letterhead paper, you can change the page format to produce the required number of lines or top margin automatically.
- If you generally print your text with a ragged-right format (rather than justified), you can change the *print format* to turn justification off.

To customize WordPerfect, you must change the default parameters on the main WordPerfect disk. In general, you should prepare and label a separate Word-Perfect disk for each format you use often. For example, you might create separate WordPerfect disks for formal correspondence, memoranda, and reports. To do this, prepare a working copy for each format (see "Copy the files" in the Word-Perfect Installation manual), then tailor the copies.

```
Set-up Menu
0 - End Set-up and enter WP

1 - Set Directories or Drives for Dictionary and Thesaurus Files
2 - Set Initial Settings
3 - Set Screen Size
4 - Set Backup Options
5 - Set Beep Options

Selection:

Press Cancel to ignore changes and return to DOS
```

Fig. 11-1. The Set-up menu.

Hard disk users may want to create a separate subdirectory for each unique format. LETTERS, MEMOS, and REPORTS would be suitable names for these subdirectories.

To customize a WordPerfect disk, put it in drive A and enter **a:wp/s** (instead of the usual **a:wp**). This makes WordPerfect display its Set-up menu, as shown in Fig. 11-1.

To change the line, page, or print format, press **2** to select *Set Initial Settings.* This makes the Change Initial Settings menu appear (see Fig. 11-2). To

```
Change Initial Settings

Press any of the keys listed below to change initial settings

Key                   Initial Settings.

Line Format           Tabs, E-Tabs, Margins, Spacing, Hy-
                      phenation, Align Character
Page Format           Page # Pos, Page Length, Top Mar-
                      gin, Page # Col Pos, W/O
Print Format          Pitch, Font, Lines/Inch, Right Just, Un-
                      derlining, SF Bin
Print                 Printer, Copies, Binding Width
Date                  Date Format
Insert/Typeover       Insert/Typeover Mode
Mark Text             Paragraph Number Definition
Footnote              Footnote/Endnote Options
Escape                Set N
Screen                Set Auto-rewrite
```

Fig. 11-2. The Change Initial Settings menu.

select from this menu, you must press the keys that correspond to the option you want to change. Here is a list of those keys:

Option	Keys
Line Format	Shift-F8
Page Format	Alt-F8
Print Format	Ctrl-F8
Print	Shift-F7
Date	Shift-F5
Insert/Typeover	Ins
Mark Text	Alt-F5
Footnote	Ctrl-F7
Escape	Esc
Screen	Ctrl-F3

CHANGING THE LINE FORMAT

To change the line format, press Shift-F8 to do a Line Format command. WordPerfect displays its Line Format menu. The changes you may want to make are:

1. *Different tabs* (option 1). WordPerfect's default tabs are at every fifth column. To add a tab, type its column number and press Enter; to delete one, move the cursor to it and press Del; to delete all tabs, press Ctrl and End.
2. *Different margins* (option 3). WordPerfect's default margins are at columns 10 and 74. To get shorter or longer lines, type new values and press Enter after each one.
3. *Different spacing* (option 4). The default value of 1 makes WordPerfect print single-spaced. To get double or triple-spacing, change it to 2 or 3. To get space-and-a-half spacing, change it to 1.5.

CHANGING THE PAGE FORMAT

To change the page format, press Alt-F8 to do a Page Format command. WordPerfect displays its Page Format menu. Generally, you only want to preset three parameters on this menu: Page Length, Top Margin, and Widow/Orphan (options 4, 5, and A).

Page Length

This parameter tells WordPerfect how long your paper is (in sixths of an inch) and how many single-spaced lines to put on it. The original values, *66* and *54*, are for standard 11-inch paper. To print on 14-inch legal-size paper, enter **2** to select *84* and *72*.

Top Margin

This parameter tells WordPerfect how many half-lines to skip before it starts to print. The original value, *12*, makes it skip one inch. To produce a two-inch top margin, enter **24**.

Widow/Orphan

This parameter tells WordPerfect how to arrange paragraphs on a page. The original value, *N*, makes it fill each page to capacity. *Y* makes it keep the first and last two lines of paragraphs together on a page. With *Y*, WordPerfect will not end a page with the first line of a paragraph, nor will it begin a page with the last line of a paragraph.

CHANGING THE PRINT FORMAT

To change the print format, press Ctrl-F8 to do a Print Format command. WordPerfect displays its Print Format menu. This menu lets you change the pitch, font, and lines per inch, and lets you turn justification on or off.

Pitch and Font

WordPerfect assumes your printer uses 10-pitch (pica) type, so it makes the default pitch *10*. To use a different type size, press **1** and enter the characters per inch value you want. To get proportional spacing (assuming your printer can produce it), type an asterisk after the number. For dot matrix printers, 10* produces pica type with proportional spacing; daisy wheel or thimble type printers often require 3* for the Pitch value. To see what each of your printer's fonts produces, print the PRINTER.TST file on the Learning disk. To obtain a list of your printers and fonts from within WordPerfect, give a Print command and select *Printer Control* and then *Display Printers and Fonts*.

Lines Per Inch

WordPerfect assumes you want 6 lines per inch, but you may change it to 8. You could do this to print with a small type size—say, 16.5 characters per inch.

Right Justification

The original setting, *On*, makes WordPerfect produce even right-hand margins by inserting spaces between words. If you generally print with a ragged right-hand margin, press **3** to switch to *Turn off*.

HINTS

For most writing on standard paper with no letterhead, I recommend the following defaults:

- Using the Line Format option, change the *Spacing* value to 2 for double-spaced text.
- Using the *Page Format* option, change *Widow/Orphan Protect* to *Y*.
- Using the *Print Format* option, turn off the justification if you want text printed with a ragged-right margin.

KEY POINT SUMMARY

The Line Format, Page Format, and Print Format defaults determine what values WordPerfect uses when you turn the power on. You can change these default settings by selecting *Set Initial Settings* from the Set-up menu. To obtain the Set-up menu, start WordPerfect by entering **a:wp/s**.

The original Line Format settings are:

- Tabs: At every fifth column (5, 10, 15, and so on).
- Margins: Columns 10 and 74
- Spacing: 1 (single-spacing)

The original Page Format settings are:

- Page Length: 66 (for 11-inch paper)
- Lines per page: 54 (for 11-inch paper)
- Top Margin: 12 (skip one inch)
- Widow/Orphan Protect: N (allow widow and orphan lines)

The original Print Format settings are:

- Pitch: 10 (i.e., 10 characters per inch, or pica), with no proportional spacing
- Font: 1
- Lines per Inch: 6
- Right Justification: On
- Underline Style: Noncontinuous Single (tabs are not underlined)

You can look up the parameters I have not mentioned in the WordPerfect manual.

Chapter 12

Using Other Programs With WordPerfect

Throughout this book we have been treating WordPerfect documents as complete and final products. In practice, you may want to combine a document with a financial report generated by a spreadsheet or a list obtained from a database.

If every computer program produced results in the same form, you could simply copy material between them. For example, you could use WordPerfect's Retrieve command to copy a Lotus 1-2-3 spreadsheet directly into a report you are writing. Alas, things aren't that easy.

Spreadsheet programs generally produce results in a different form than word processing programs. Likewise, database programs produce results in a different form than spreadsheets or word processors. Thus, in general, most programs are incompatible.

Fortunately, WordPerfect includes a program that can convert the results of various kinds of programs into WordPerfect documents. Conversely, it can also convert WordPerfect documents into a form that can be used by another program. This chapter describes the conversion procedure. It also includes examples of using the results of spreadsheets and databases with WordPerfect.

FILE CONVERSION

WordPerfect contains a special program called CONVERT that can convert material from one format to another. To use it, start your computer as usual and obtain the B> prompt, then proceed as follows:

1. Insert the Learning disk into drive A and insert the disk that has the file to be converted into drive B.
2. Enter **a:convert**. This produces a copyright notice, then the prompt *Name of Input File?*
3. Enter the name of the file you want to convert. For a computer with floppy disks, the name should be of the form **b:filename**. With a hard disk, enter just the name if the file is in the WordPerfect subdirectory (e.g., enter **report.doc**). If it is in a different subdirectory, precede the file name with a \, the subdirectory name, and another \ (e.g., \ **mm** \ **report.doc** specifies the report.doc file in a MultiMate subdirectory).
4. When the prompt *Name of Output File?* appears, enter the name you want the converted file to have (it cannot be the same as the original name). This makes the Convert menu (Fig. 12-1) appear.
5. Type the number that corresponds to the format of your original (Input) file.

Option 1 (WordPerfect) lets you convert a WordPerfect document to any of five formats. They are:

- *Revisable-Form-Text* is the DCA (Document Content Architecture) format used by large IBM mainframe computers.
- *Navy DIF* (for Data Interchange Format) is a U.S. Navy spreadsheet format.
- *WordStar* is the format used by MicroPro International Corporation's word processor.
- *MultiMate* is the format used by Multimate International's MultiMate and MultiMate Advantage word processors.
- *Seven-bit transfer format* is used by modems (devices that transfer data over telephone lines).

Option 8 (WordPerfect Secondary Merge) is similar, but it works with secondary merge files rather than regular WordPerfect documents. Specifically, it con-

```
        1 WordPerfect
        2 Revisable-Form-Text (DCA - IBM Mainframe DISOSS Format)
        3 Navy DIF Standard
        4 WordStar
        5 MultiMate
        6 Seven-bit transfer format
        7 Mail Merge
        8 WordPerfect Secondary Merge
        9 Spreadsheet DIF

        Enter number indicating input file type:
```

Fig. 12-1. The Convert menu.

verts a secondary file to the DIF formats that many spreadsheet programs (including Lotus 1-2-3) use to represent numerical data. In the converted file, records become rows and fields become entries, or *cells.*

The remaining options convert various kinds of program files to WordPerfect, as follows:

- Options 2 through 5 convert DCA, Navy DIF, WordStar, and MultiMate files to WordPerfect format.
- Option 6 restores a previously converted WordPerfect file from seven-bit transfer format (see option 1) to its original form.
- Option 7 (Mail Merge) converts files to secondary merge format. It can operate on WordStar Mail Merge files or on files produced by Ashton-Tate's popular dBASE II and dBASE III database management programs.
- Option 9 (Spreadsheet DIF) does the opposite of option 8. That is, it converts a spreadsheet DIF file to secondary merge format. In the converted file, rows become records and cells become fields.

ELECTRONIC SPREADSHEETS

Without a doubt, the most popular business program is the electronic spreadsheet. If your reports involve tables of numbers requiring arithmetic manipulation, an electronic spreadsheet can save you a lot of hand calculations.

To explain what an electronic spreadsheet does, let us consider a practical application. Suppose you own a clothing store and want to find out how your business is doing. You could take a large piece of paper and rule it off into rows and columns. Each row would correspond to a different department: men's suits, children's wear, sportswear, women's fashions, and so on.

The first 12 columns would be monthly sales totals, followed by yearly totals, comparisons with previous months or previous years, commissions, sales taxes, and so forth. You could add down the monthly columns (giving monthly totals) and add across the rows (giving annual totals for a given department). You could also figure annual receipts, net profits (receipts minus costs), and other results.

How would you do this by hand? You would enter the numbers from your account books and use a calculator to add each row and column, one after the other. Surely, this would be a long, tedious, error-prone task. The electronic spreadsheet can do all the calculations simultaneously. It lets you label rows and columns and tell the computer how they are related.

For example, you could label the monthly columns with the names of the months. You could then specify that the Yearly Total column is the sum of the monthly columns. Similarly, you could say that the Monthly Cost row is the sum of all departmental costs for a particular month. After you tell the computer what the rows and columns mean, you enter your data.

The computer quickly and automatically performs all the calculations at once.

It's like having many calculators, each doing its specific task and passing its results on if other calculators need them. You can also change any number on the spreadsheet, and the program will instantly recalculate everything the number affects.

You can copy the results of a spreadsheet such as Lotus' 1-2-3 or Microsoft's Multiplan into a WordPerfect document. For example, you might be preparing a loan proposal to a bank for a possible expansion of your clothing store. To begin, you develop a spreadsheet that lists income, costs, and profits for the last five years and uses them to make five-year projections under reasonable assumptions about inflation rates, profit margins, operating costs, and so forth.

You save this spreadsheet as a DIF file on your data disk and then use the CONVERT program's *Spreadsheet DIF* option (9) to convert it to a WordPerfect document. When you reach the point where the spreadsheet is to appear, copy it into the loan proposal document with a Retrieve command. After that, you can reformat, expand, or otherwise change the spreadsheet just as you would change standard WordPerfect text.

An electronic spreadsheet is a great timesaver for an accountant, banker, insurance agent, purchasing manager, sales manager, broker, or anyone else who works with figures. Furthermore, it ensures greater accuracy and allows the user to calculate more results and try out variables such as inflation, interest rates, market penetration, or foreign exchange rates.

Lotus 1-2-3 Procedure

Lotus 1-2-3 produces spreadsheets in its own unique format called WKS (for worksheet, which is what Lotus Development Corp. calls a spreadsheet). WordPerfect cannot convert the WKS format directly, but the 1-2-3 program contains a procedure to convert a WKS file to a DIF file—and DIF is a format WordPerfect can handle. Hence, we must make two separate conversions: WKS to DIF (using 1-2-3) and then DIF to WordPerfect (using WordPerfect). The procedure is as follows:

1. Start 1-2-3 as usual.
2. Create the worksheet or load it in from disk with a /File Retrieve command.
3. Put your WordPerfect data disk in drive B.
4. Select /File Xtract and then Formulas.
5. When 1-2-3 asks for the Xtract filename, enter **b:** and the name you want to give the file. (For example, **b:salespro** would be suitable for a table of sales projections.)
6. When 1-2-3 asks for the Xtract range, enter the beginning column and row, two periods, the ending column and row, and then press Return. For example, to extract rows 6 through 24 of columns A through G, enter **A6..G24**.
7. When the top right-hand corner of the screen shows *:READY:*, select /Quit and Yes to leave 1-2-3.
8. When the Lotus Access System command menu appears, select Translate,

then choose WKS to DIF.

9. For the source disk drive, specify B.
10. When the computer asks you to *Select file for processing*, use the down-arrow key to highlight the filename you entered in step 5, then press Return.
11. For the destination disk drive, specify B.
12. Select *Yes* to proceed with the translation.
13. When the screen shows *Press any key to clear display and continue*, press Return.
14. When the File Translation System menu reappears, select *Quit* and *Yes*.
15. When the Lotus Access System command menu appears, select *Exit* and *Yes* to leave Lotus.

Your data disk now contains two versions of the worksheet, one in Lotus 1-2-3 worksheet format (e.g., SALESPRO.WKS) and another in DIF format (e.g., SALESPRO.DIF). To convert the DIF file to a WordPerfect document, do the following:

1. Put your WordPerfect Learning disk in drive A, replacing the Lotus disk, and enter **a:convert**.
2. When the *Name of Input File?* prompt appears, enter the filename and **.dif** (e.g., enter **salespro.dif**).
3. When the *Name of Output File?* prompt appears, enter the same filename, but give it a different extension. Since the result will be a secondary merge file, *.sf* is a reasonable choice (e.g., enter **salespro.sf**).
4. When the Convert menu appears, type **9** to select *Spreadsheet DIF*.

Once you have converted a spreadsheet to a WordPerfect file, you can copy it into any other document using the regular Retrieve command.

Using Wide Spreadsheets

A problem with spreadsheets is that they are often wider than your paper. (For example, Lotus 1-2-3 provides 2,048 rows and 254 columns!) To use a wide spreadsheet, set up margins for it, Retrieve it and then distribute it over several pages with column move and copy operations; see "Column Operations" in Chapter 6.

DATABASE MANAGEMENT PROGRAMS

Database management programs let you create, search, sort, combine, and perform arithmetic operations on lists of text and numbers. For example, you could enter purchase orders into a database, and then have it produce a list of customers who bought more than, say, 100 units in the last year. Or you could make the database produce a file of customers in a given state, sorted by city.

Producing Form Letters from Database Files

In Chapter 10 I described how to produce form letters with WordPerfect. To do this, you must merge a generalized copy of the letter (primary file) with a data file (secondary merge file) containing the items you want to insert—name, address, account status, etc. Let us now describe how to use a data file produced by dBASE II, the popular database management program from Ashton-Tate.

Suppose you have a dBASE II file called CUSTMRS that holds current information about your company's customers. Each entry, or *record,* in the file has the following format:

> company, street, city, state, zipcode, indtype, buyer, salutation, telephone, salesyr, region

At the beginning of a new year, you want to write a letter offering special terms to each customer who bought at least $100,000 worth of goods last year. You must select these customers' records from the dBASE II file.

To begin, start dBASE II and enter the following commands to select the qualifying customers (assuming your data files are on drive B):

```
USE B:CUSTMRS
COPY TO B:BIGSLS.DB FOR SALESYR > = 100000 DELIMITED WITH ,
QUIT
```

The dBASE II commands and qualifiers here have the following meanings:

- *USE B:CUSTMRS* specifies which database file dBASE II is to use.
- *COPY* copies from the database in USE to another file.
- *TO B:BIGSLS.DB* assigns the name of the new file (DB stands for database).
- *FOR SALESYR > = 100000* selects records with yearly sales greater than or equal to 100000: > = means greater than or equal to.
- *DELIMITED WITH ,* separates fields with commas.
- *QUIT* makes the computer leave dBASE II.

The entries in the BIGSLS.DB file will look like the following:

> Bay Tea Co.,105 Federal Ave.,Boston,MA,01284,Food,Mr. Thomas Wheaton,Tom,617-555-1776,123000,NE
> XYZ Computers,34 Lake Rd.,Big Palm,FL,32650,Computer,Ms. Carrie Raye,Carrie,904-987-2854,140000,SE

This represents two records, one for Bay Tea Co. and another for XYZ Computers.

Now you must convert the BIGSLS.DB file to WordPerfect's secondary merge file format. Do this as follows:

1. Put your WordPerfect Learning disk in drive A, replacing the dBASE disk, and enter **a:convert**.
2. When the *Name of Input File?* prompt appears, enter **bigsls.db**.
3. When the *Name of Output File?* prompt appears, enter **bigsls.sf** (for secondary file.
4. When the Convert menu appears, type **7** to select *Mail Mqerge*.
5. CONVERT now needs some information about the makeup of your database file. When it asks for the *Field delimiter*, enter , (i.e., type a comma and press Enter). When it asks for the *Record delimiter*, enter **{13}{10}**. When it asks for the *Characters to be stripped from file*, press Enter.

```
                              November 6, 1986

^F7^
^F1^
^F2^
^F3^,  ^F4^  ^F5^

Dear ^F8^:

    We are pleased to inform you that your company has qualified
for our 1986 Special Discount Progr_m.  As a valued customer, you
are entitled to the following privileges:

1) 45-day terms on all purchases.

2) An extra 2% discount in advance, as well as our usual 2%
   discount for payments made within 15 days.

3) Free returns (you pay shipping costs only) on all goods
   unsold after 90 days.

We appreciate your patronage and plan to do all we can to
continue this important relationship.

                              Sincerely,



                              Ray Cornell
                              National Sales Manager
^T^N^P^P
```

Fig. 12-2. The form letter to be sent to customer list selected by dBASE II.

Finally, you can prepare the primary merge file—the letter you want to send to the BIGSLS customer list. This letter is shown in Fig. 12-2. (Note that the ^Fn^ numbers assume you know the order of the fields in the database file. If you aren't sure of this order, enter **DISPLAY STRUCTURE** while in dBASE II to obtain it.) When you finish the letter, do a Merge command to print the copies.

TEXT FILES

Most computers transfer information internally as pure text. The WordPerfect manual refers to this format as a *DOS text*; some other manuals call it *AS-CII*, short for "American Standard Code for Information Interchange." DOS text is, in essence, the generic computer format. Nearly every program can both read text information and produce text results. Thus, you would use DOS text to communicate with programs that cannot produce any of the formats that CONVERT can use. For example, you would work with it to use documents produced by a non-CONVERTible word processor.

To transfer a DOS text file to or from WordPerfect, press Ctrl-F5 to do a Text In/Out command. This produces the menu shown in Fig. 12-3. Options 1 and 2 are, of course, used to save or retrieve the text file.

Locking and Unlocking Documents

Options 3 and 4 of the Text In/Out menu let you *lock* and *unlock* documents. This is a security feature. A locked document is one to which you assign a password. After that, no one (not even you!) can Retrieve the document unless they first unlock it by entering the password.

To lock and save the current document, choose option 3. When WordPerfect shows *Enter Password:*, enter a password of up to 75 characters. (Note that the password does not appear on the screen.) When it shows *Re-enter Password:*, enter the same password again. Finally, save the document as usual.

To retrieve a locked document, choose option 4. When WordPerfect shows *Document to be Retrieved:*, enter its name. When *Enter password:* appears, enter the password you used to lock the document. This makes the document appear on the screen. The password is still in effect, however; when you save the document (even with the regular Save or Exit command), WordPerfect requires you to enter it.

Document Conversion and Locking

1 - Save current document as a DOS text file
2 - Retrieve a DOS text file
3 - Lock and save current document
4 - Unlock and retrieve a locked document

Fig. 12-3. The Text In/Out menu.

Note that the password system is permanent; you can only get rid of it by deleting the document or Blocking the entire document and then saving the block as a regular file. Therefore, be very selective in deciding which documents to lock. Don't lock anything unless it's absolutely necessary. Finally, choose your password carefully, make it easy to remember (say, use your Social Security number), and use the same password for every document you lock.

Appendix A

WordPerfect Commands

Advance Down	Shift-F1, 5
Advance Line	Shift-F1, 6
Advance Up	Shift-F1, 4
Align Character	Shift-F8, 6
Alt Key Mapping	Ctrl-F3, 3
Append Block	Alt-F4, Ctrl-F4, 3
Auto Rewrite	Ctrl-F3, 5
Binding Width	Shift-F7, 3, 3
Block	Alt-F4
Bold	F6
Cancel	F1
Cancel Merge Operation	Shift-F9
Cancel Print Job(s)	Shift-F7, 4, A
Center	Shift-F6
Center Page Top to Bottom	Alt-F8, 3
Change Directory	F5, Enter, 7
Change Print Options	Shift-F7, 3
Colors	Ctrl-F3, 4
Columns, text	Alt-F7, 3 (On/Off) or 4 (Def)
Conditional End of Page	Alt-F8, 9

Copy	Ctrl-F4
Block	Alt-F4, Ctrl-F4, 2
Column	Alt-F4, Ctrl-F4, 4
File	F5, Enter, 8
Page	Ctrl-F4, 3, 2
Paragraph	Ctrl-F4, 2, 2
Rectangle	Alt-F4, Ctrl-F4, 5
Sentence	Ctrl-F4, 1, 2
Ctrl Key Mapping	Ctrl-F3, 3
Cut (Move)	
Block	Alt-F4, Ctrl-F4, 1
Column	Alt-F4, Ctrl-F4, 4
Page	Ctrl-F4, 3, 1
Paragraph	Ctrl-F4, 2, 1
Rectangle	Alt-F4, Ctrl-F4, 5
Sentence	Ctrl-F4, 1, 1
Date	Shift-F5
Define Macro	Ctrl-F10
Define Style	Alt-F5, 6
Delete	
Block	Alt-F4, Del
Character	Del (current) or Backspace (preceding)
End of Line	Ctrl-End
End of Page	Ctrl-PgDn
File	F5, Enter, 2
Page	Ctrl-F4, 3, 1
Paragraph	Ctrl-F4, 2, 1
Sentence	Ctrl-F4, 1, 1
Word	Ctrl-Backspace
Display All Print Jobs	Shift-F7, 4, D
Display Printers and Fonts	Shift-F7, 4, 2
Draw Line	Ctrl-F3, 2
End of Page, Conditional	Alt-F8, 9
Endnote	Ctrl-F7, 5 (Create) or 6 (Edit)
Escape	Esc
Exit and Save Document	F7
Extended Tab Set	Shift-F8, 2
Flush Right	Alt-F6
Font	Ctrl-F8, 1
Fonts, Display	Shift-F7, 4, 2
Footers	Alt-F8, 6

Footnote	Ctrl-F7
Generate	Alt-F5, 7
Go (Resume Printing)	Shift-F7, 4, G
Headers	Alt-F8, 6
Help	F3
Hyphenation	Shift-F8, 5
Indent	F4
Indent, Left	Shift-F4
Index	Alt-F5, 5
Index, mark for	Alt-4, Alt-5, 5
Justification, Right	Ctrl-F8, 3 (off) or 4 (on)
Line Draw	Ctrl-F3, 2
List, mark for	Alt-F4, Alt-F5, 2
List Files	F5, Enter
Line Format	Shift-F8
Lines per Inch	Ctrl-F8, 2
Look at (View) File	F5, Enter, 6
Macro, Define	Ctrl-F10
Macro, Start	Alt-F10
Margins	Shift-F8, 3
Mark Block	Alt-F4, Alt-F5
Mark Text	Alt-F5
Math	Alt-F7, 1 (On) or 2 (Def)
Merge	Ctrl-F9, 1
Merge, cancel	Shift-F9
Merge Codes	Alt-F9
Merge E (^E)	Shift-F9
Merge R (^R)	F9
Move	Ctrl-F4
Block	Alt-F4, Ctrl-F4, 1
Column	Alt-F4, Ctrl-F4, 4
Page	Ctrl-F4, 3, 1
Paragraph	Ctrl-F4, 2, 1
Rectangle	Alt-F4, Ctrl-F4, 5
Sentence	Ctrl-F4, 1, 1
New Page	Ctrl-Enter

New Page Number	Alt-F8, 2
Number of Copies	Shift-F7, 3, 2
Outline	Alt-F5, 1
Overstrike	Shift-F1, 3
Page	
Format	Alt-F8
Format, Suppress	Alt-F8, 8
Length	Alt-F8, 4
New	Ctrl-Enter
Number Column Positions	Alt-F8, 7
Number Position	Alt-F8, 1
Print	Shift-F7, 2
Paragraph Numbers, insert	Alt-F5, 2
Pitch	Ctrl-F8, 1
Print	Shift-F7
Block	Alt-F4, Shift-F7
Current Document	Shift-F7, 1
Disk Document	Shift-F7, 4, P or F5, Enter, 4
Format	Ctrl-F8
Job(s), Cancel	Shift-F7, 4, A
Jobs, Display All	Shift-F7, 4, D
Options, Change	Shift-F7, 3
Options, Select	Shift-F7, 4, 1
Page	Shift-F7, 2
Printer Control	Shift-F7, 4
Printer Number	Shift-F7, 3, 1
Printers, Display	Shift-F7, 4, 2
Printers, Select	Shift-F7, 4, 3
Printing, Resume (Go)	Shift-F7, 4, G
Printing, Stop	Shift-F7, 4, S
Proportional Spacing	Ctrl-F8, 1
Redline	Alt-F5, 3
Redline, mark for	Alt-4, Alt-5, 3
Remove Redline or Strikeout	Alt-F5, 4
Rename File	F5, Enter, 3
Replace	Alt-F2
Resume Printing (Go)	Shift-F7, 4, G
Retrieve	
Column (Move)	Ctrl-F4, 4
File	Shift-F10 or F5, Enter, 1
Rectangle (Move)	Ctrl-F4, 6

Text (Move)	Ctrl-F4, 5
	Ctrl-F3, 0
Rewrite Screen	Alt-F3
Reveal Codes	Ctrl-F8, 3 (off) or 4 (on)
Right Justification	Shift-F7, 4, R
Rush Print Job	
Save	F10
Save and Exit	F7
Search Backward	Shift-F2
Search Forward	F2
Screen	Ctrl-F3
Screen Colors	Ctrl-F3, 4
Select Print Options	Shift-F7, 4, 1
Select Printers	Shift-F7, 4, 3
Shell	Ctrl-F1
Sort	Ctrl-F9, 2
Sorting Sequences	Ctrl-F9, 3
Spacing	Shift-F8, 4
Spell	Ctrl-F2
Start Macro	Alt-F10
Stop Printing	Shift-F7, 4, S
Strikeout, mark for	Alt-4, Alt-5, 4
Subscript	Shift-F1, 2
Superscript	Shift-F1, 1
Suppress Page Format	Alt-F8, 8
Switch Windows	Shift-F3
Tab Align	Ctrl-F6
Tab Set	Shift-F8, 1
Table of Contents, mark for	Alt-F4, Alt-F5, 1
Text In/Out	Ctrl-F5
Text File in	F5, Enter, 5
Thesaurus	Alt-F1
Top Margin	Alt-F8, 5
Typeover On/Off	Ins
Type-thru	Shift-F7, 5
Undelete	F1
Underline	F8
Widow/Orphan Protect	Alt-F8, A
Window	Ctrl-F3, 1
Word Count	Ctrl-F2, 6
Word Search	F5, Enter, 9

Common DOS Operations

You will occasionally want to do some general "housekeeping" work on disks that contain WordPerfect documents. For example, you may want to copy an entire disk or a single document, or give a document a new name that is easier to remember. You can do some of these operations from within WordPerfect, using the List Files command (F5), but it is often quicker and easier to do them from DOS. This appendix describes common DOS operations; for others or more details, refer to the IBM DOS manual.

STARTING DOS

To begin, insert the IBM DOS disk in the left-hand drive (A) and switch the power on. Type the appropriate responses and press Enter when the computer asks for the date and time. The $A>$ tells you the computer is waiting for a DOS command. If you want to do something that involves one disk (e.g., delete a file or format a disk), put the disk in the right-hand drive (B). If you want to do something that involves two disks (e.g., copy a disk), replace the DOS disk with the source disk and put the second disk in drive B.

FILENAMES

WordPerfect lets you give every disk file a name of up to eight characters, plus a three letter *extension* that describes what kind of information the file contains. For example, you may give letters the extension .LET, reports the extension .RPT, and so on.

When operating on a file using a DOS command, you must enter both its name and its extension. For example, to operate on the document SALES.RPT, you would enter **SALES.RPT**. Furthermore, you must put the drive name (A:, B:, or C:) in front of the filename if the file is not on the active drive. Hence, you would enter **B:SALES.RPT** if A is the active drive and SALES.RPT is in B.

Finally, if you are working from a hard disk (usually drive C) and the file is not in the active directory, you must put the path in front of the filename. Hence, you would enter **C:\REPORTS\SALES.RPT** if SALES.RPT is in the REPORTS directory. The combination of drive name, path, filename, and extension is referred to as a *file specification* or *filespec*.

Operating on Groups of Files

DOS lets you operate on entire groups of similarly named files. You can, for example, copy or display a directory of a group of files with a single command. The way to do this is with *wildcard* characters that act as shorthand for "any character" or "any group of characters." You can compare them with the Joker in popular card games, a free number in Bingo, or a blank tile in Scrabble.

The character *?* means "any single character." You can put *?* anywhere in a filename—even several times. For example, the command

    DIR RPTQ28?.RPT

displays a list (directory) of report files for all second-quarter sales reports for the 1980s. Similarly, the command

    DIR RPTQ?8?.RPT

displays a list of all quarterly sales reports for the 1980s.

The * (asterisk) is an even more all-encompassing wildcard. It tells DOS that any character can occupy that position and all remaining positions in the filename or extension. For example, the command

    DIR RPTQ*.RPT

displays all RPTQ report files, regardless of their quarter or year. Similarly, the command

    DIR RPTQ*.*

displays all files whose names begin with RPTQ, regardless of their extension.

COMMON DOS COMMANDS

Table B-1 summarizes the common DOS commands. Here, items in brackets are optional.

Table B-1. Common DOS Commands.

Command	Action	Comments
CHKDSK [d:]	Displays a disk and memory status report.	
COPY old-filespec [new-filespec]	Copies files.	
DIR [filespec]	Displays name, size, date, and time of file(s) on disk.	If you omit the filespec, DIR summarizes the entire disk.
DISKCOPY source-drive target-drive	Copies an entire disk.	Target disk need not be formatted.
ERASE filespec	Delete files.	
FORMAT [d:]	Prepares a disk to accept DOS files.	Deletes any files currently on the disk
RENAME old-filespec new-filespec	Changes a file's name.	

The COPY Command

As you might expect, COPY copies files. If you copy them onto another disk, you can give them the same names as the originals. If you copy files onto the same disk or into the same disk directory, you must rename them. Either way, COPY does not affect the original files.

COPY obviously requires two filespecs—a source and a destination; the source comes first. You may omit the destination's name if it is the same as the source's. The following command copies SALES.RPT from drive A to drive B:

COPY SALES.RPT B:

You might also want to copy all document files to a new disk for backup. If you named them with a .DOC extension, copy them with

COPY *.DOC B:

Finally, you might want to copy a document to use as a starting point for preparing a new document. For example, the following command makes a copy of 1986's sales report as a starting point for preparing 1987's:

```
COPY SALES86.RPT SALES87.RPT
```

The DIRectory Command

DIR displays the following information about files on a disk: filename and extension, size in characters, and the date and time it was most recently saved. A typical entry looks like this:

```
REPORT86 DOC 1920 5-29-86 9:45p
```

This tells you that REPORT86 has the extension DOC and is 1920 characters long. 5-29-86 (May 29, 1986) is the date on which you most recently saved REPORT86.DOC. 9:45 p.m. (long day!) is the time when you saved it. Obviously, these are correct only if you entered the time and date when DOS asked you for them.

You can follow DIR with a filespec. This limits the display to files in a particular group. Typical examples are:

```
DIR                 (Display all files on the active drive.)
DIR B:              (Display all files on drive B.)
DIR B:*.DOC         (Display all DOC files on drive B.)
DIR B:NEW*.DOC      (Same, but display only DOC files whose file-
                    names start with NEW.)
```

If your disk has many files, the display may move up the screen so fast that you can't read it. To stop the scrolling temporarily, press Ctrl and Num Lock. To stop the scrolling altogether, press Ctrl and Break simultaneously.

The CHecK DiSK Command

CHKDSK tells you how many files a disk contains and how many bytes (characters) are unused. It also reports on memory use. CHKDSK reports on the active disk unless you follow it with a drive name.

A typical report from CHKDSK looks like this:

```
362496 bytes total disk space
350000 bytes in 12 user files
 12496 bytes available on disk

655360 bytes total memory
386672 bytes free
```

The top lines tell you the disk's status. This particular disk is nearly full, since only 12,496 bytes of its 362,496-byte capacity are still available. If any of the files on the disk are more than, say, 10,000 bytes long (as indicated by a DIR command), you should switch to a new disk to avoid WordPerfect's *Disk full* message.

As a rule of thumb, when a data disk has less than 20,000 bytes available, you should change disks. Disks are inexpensive, and you do not want to lose some work because a disk is full.

The DISKCOPY Command

DISKCOPY copies an entire disk. The general form is:

DISKCOPY source-drive target-drive

Note that the source drive comes first. The target drive need not be formatted, since DOS will format it automatically before copying to it.

The ERASE Command

ERASE deletes files. It can delete a single file or a group of files. Typical examples are:

ERASE REPORT86.DOC   (Delete only REPORT86.DOC.)
ERASE REPORT.*   (Delete every REPORT file.)
ERASE B:NEW*.DOC   (Delete DOC files that begin with NEW.)

Be careful if you use ? and * to erase a group of files, because a single misplaced character may result in the deletion of files you want to keep. To avoid disaster, run DIR with the filespec you plan to use with ERASE. This will provide a list of all files that ERASE will delete.

The FORMAT Command

FORMAT prepares a disk to accept DOS files, including WordPerfect files. You can compare formatting a disk with drawing lines on a baseball or football field or marking the origins and axes on a piece of graph paper. That is, formatting prepares the disk for use but doesn't actually do anything with it.

You can follow FORMAT with a drive name to specify the disk to be formatted, as in

FORMAT B:

This is the form you would normally use to prepare a new WordPerfect document disk. Always be certain that your new disk is in the drive specified, because an accidental FORMAT of a working disk will destroy all data on it.

The RENAME Command

RENAME changes a file's name. This command obviously requires two filespecs; the old one comes first. For example, the command

RENAME B:SALESRPT.BK! OLDSALES

changes the name of SALESRPT.BK! on drive B to OLDSALES. That is, it converts a backup file into a regular WordPerfect document file.

RENAME can also preserve files while you are deleting an entire group. For example, suppose you have documents named SALES83, SALES84, SALES85, and SALES86. If you want to delete all except SALES86, you can do so with the sequence

RENAME SALES86 TEMP
ERASE SALES*
RENAME TEMP SALES86

Here, TEMP serves as a temporary "hideout" for SALES86, keeping it from being ERASEd.

Index

Index

80340

Other Bestsellers From TAB

☐ **LOTUS® 1-2-3® SIMPLIFIED—2nd Edition, including Version 2.0—Bolocan**

A book that guides you painlessly from the most basic computer and spreadsheet operations right through the most advanced and powerful operations of 2.0—all in easy-to-follow, logical sequence. Lotus 1-2-3 Version 2.0 is considered one of the most versatile and powerful business software packages available. With this hands-on guide, it can also be one of the easiest to use! 272 pp., 207 illus. 7" × 10".

Paper $14.95   **Hard $21.95**
Book No. 2748

☐ **PROGRAMMING WITH dBASE III® PLUS—Prague and Hammitt**

Packed will expect programming techniques and shortcuts, this is an essential guide to Ashton Tate's newest version of its dBASE relational database manager for the IBM® PC™. It includes all the practical, use-it-now advice and guidance beginning PC users are looking for . . . as well as power programming techniques that will allow more advanced users to increase productivity while sharply reducing application development time. Exceptionally well documented and packed with program examples—including a sophisticated payroll and inventory system—this is a sourcebook that goes well beyond material covered in ordinary user's manuals. 384 pp., 150 illus., 7" × 10".

Paper $21.95   **Hard $29.95**
Book No. 2726

☐ **FRAMEWORK II™—Prague and Kasevich**

If you're looking for expert guidance on tapping the full potential offered by the new Framework II package, this is your answer! Here's all the hands-on, nontechnical explanations that you need to take command of Framework II's combined functions of spreadsheet, database, graphics, and communications programming. Plus there's a series of programs to help explain Framework II's important programming features. 384 pp., 335 illus. 7" × 10".

Paper $21.95   **Hard $29.95**
Book No. 2716

☐ **PRACTICAL GUIDE TO THE BPI™ ACCOUNTING SYSTEM—Flanagan**

Includes a wealth of practical operating tips and techniques that give you the know-how you need to make a BPI accounting module on your IBM PC, Apple, NEC™, or other micro as effective and efficient as possible! Covers all of the basic BPI accounting modules—general accounting, accounts payable, accounts receivable, job cost, inventory, and payroll, 224 pp., 39 illus. 7" × 10".

Paper $14.95   **Hard $21.95**
Book No. 2696

☐ **INCREASING PRODUCTIVITY WITH PFS® AND THE IBM® ASSISTANT SERIES—2nd Edition—Burton**

Shows how to get more applications power from all 7 PFS modules—PFS:Plan, PFS:Report, PFS:Graph, PFS:Proof, PFS:Access, PFS:File, and PFS:Write, and comparable IBM Assistant Series modules. Focuses on real world business applications with ten separate templates you can use to prepare more than 20 different forms and reports. 256 pp., 210 illus. 7" × 10".

Paper $16.95   **Hard $22.95**
Book No. 2729

☐ **MASTERING SYMPHONY®—2nd Edition—Bolocan**

You'll find step-by-step instructions on the use of Symphony's windows and its powerful command language capabilities, how-tos for transporting information from one package to another, and detailed coverage of macro programming techniques. In addition, you'll benefit from expert guidance on such concepts as spreadsheet recalculation and how to use backup files effectively, and invaluable at-a-glance summaries of each Symphony command and complete definitions of key terms. 256 pp., 238 illus. Large Format 7" × 10".

Paper $16.95   **Hard $22.95**
Book No. 2718

☐ **ANALYSIS WITH REFLEX™**

This exceptional, straightforward guide shows you a totally new way to look at your data using color and/or graphics capabilities, including the IBM® PC. You'll use it for reviewing production rates; analyzing questionnaire results; producing reports and presentations; keeping and employee database; tracking sales performance by individual and product; and much more! 224 pp., 150 illus., 7" × 10".

Paper $16.95   **Hard $22.95**
Book No. 2712

☐ **SUPERCALC® 3: LEARNING, USING AND MASTERING—Willis and Pasewark**

An essential guide to mastering all the powerful, new features offered by this amazing business tool! In no time you'll be putting your IBM® PC, PCjr., Apple® IIe, or TI Pro to work in dozens of number-crunching ways using Super-Calc 3—the powerful electronic spreadsheet that lets you custom design your own program for organizing, arranging, and manipulating information. 256 pp., 125 illus. 7" × 10".

Paper $16.95   **Hard $22.95**
Book No. 2694

Other Bestsellers From TAB

☐ **THE ILLUSTRATED DICTIONARY OF MICROCOMPUTERS—2nd Edition**
Meticulously researched and thoroughly update to include all of the most recent terminology and usage related to the microcomputer industry, this is an essential sourcebook for technically and nontechnically oriented alike—businessmen, hobbyists, students, and professionals. Provides clear, concise definitions and explanations for more than 8,000 key terms—nearly twice as many as the first best-selling edition. 360 pp., 357 illus. 7″ × 10″.
Paper $14.95   **Hard $24.95**
Book No. 2688

☐ **PROGRAMMING WITH R:base® 5000—Prague and Hammitt**
Picking up where user's manuals leave off, Prague and Hammitt guide you through all the many capabilities offered by R:base 5000, and show you how to adapt these capabilities for your own applications needs. In fact, the authors cover everything from how to use basic R:base tools to using R:base 5000 as a complete programming language for writing your own applications programs. 400 pp., 266 illus. 7″ × 10″.
Paper $19.95   **Hard $28.95**
Book No. 2666

☐ **THE COMPUTER SECURITY HANDBOOK—Baker**
Electronic breaking and entering into computer systems used by business, industry and personal computerists has reached epidemic proportions. This up-to-date sourcebook provides a realistic examination of today's computer security problems, shows you how to analyze your home and business security needs, and gives you guidance in planning your own computer security system. 288 pp., 61 illus. 7″ × 10″.
Hard $25.00   **Book No. 2608**

☐ **HARVARD PROJECT MANAGER/TOTAL PROJECT MANAGER: CONTROLLING YOUR RESOURCES**
Now this excellent new sourcebook provides the answers you need to sharpen your management skills and to begin getting better use from both your IBM® PC or compatible and what is considered by most authorities to be the most advanced project management software available—*Harvard Project Manager* and *Harvard Total Project Manager!* 240 pp., 180 illus., 7″ × 10″.
Paper $16.95   **Hard $21.95**
Book No. 2678

☐ **THE MICRO TO MAINFRAME CONNECTION—Brumm**
Experienced systems analyst and software developer Penn Brumm provides data communications planners and managers with the latest information on data handling technology and how these advances can affect your own business practice. Most importantly, she provides this information in a clearly focused, easy-to-follow style that doesn't require a technical degree to understand. 224 pp., 54 illus. 7″ × 10″.
Paper $15.95   **Hard $22.95**
Book No. 2637

☐ **DATA COMMUNICATIONS AND AREA NETWORKING HANDBOOK**
With data communications and LANs being the area of greatest growth in computers, this sourcebook will help you understand what this emerging field is all about. Singled our for its depth and comprehensiveness, this clearly-written handbook will provide you with everything from data communications standards and protocols to the various ways to link together LANs. 240 pp., 209 illus., 7″ × 10″.
Hard $25.00   **Book No. 2603**

*Prices subject to change without notice.

Look for these and other TAB books at your local bookstore.

TAB BOOKS Inc.
P.O. Box 40
Blue Ridge Summit, PA 17214

Send for FREE TAB catalog describing over 1200 current titles in print.

97680044